The Poor Man's Guide to Financial Freedom

A Realistic, Ten-Step Manual for Building Liberating Wealth on a Low to Medium Income

By Nikolai Vladivostok

Money is a terrible master but an excellent servant.

- P.T. Barnum

This book does not constitute financial advice. It contains information of a general nature and does not take into account your specific circumstances. Before making any financial decisions, you should seek your own, independent financial advice to ensure they meet your unique needs and objectives.

This is not meaningless legal mumbo jumbo I've put here to cover my bottom from the litigious. In fact, there's a whole chapter on how to find and use good financial advice. It's *Step 9: Get Advice*.

Cover illustration by Mars Dorian – www.marsdorian.com

Acknowledgements

I would like to thank Adam Piggot (www.pushingrubberdownhill.com) and Timothy Buckingham for their invaluable feedback in making this book as detailed and comprehensive as it has become. If anything vital is missing, blame them.

Contents

Introduction

This book is a detailed, step-by-step instruction manual for achieving financial freedom. But what *is* that, exactly? To better understand the concept, consider the following questions:

Could you quit your job if you wanted to?

That is, could you resign tomorrow, *knowing* you would be financially secure for long enough to easily find another position? Say, for a whole year? If the answer is 'no', are you not a slave? While you may presently enjoy your work, if things took a turn for the worse you would have to continue working there for much longer than you'd like, or quit without another job lined up, which would be a huge risk.

If you played it safe and stayed on, you would have to tolerate any degree of injustice, bullying or plain stupidity, and you would have to put up with it all while keeping that pleasant, non-confrontational and submissive smile on your face.

If someone else took the credit for your hard work and initiative, or if you copped the blame for someone else's failure, or if the new boss turned out to be a psychopath, or if a customer berated you over an issue you have no authority to fix, or if the mean girls were spreading absurd rumors about you, or if your pay was late or incomplete, you would be unable to print out and sign a resignation letter, collect your things in a box, get that cute reception girl's number and stride out the door with a smirk on your face, calm as a Brahman cow.

If you can quit any time you like without risk, you are free.

This book will show you how to position yourself such that, if it ever became necessary, you would be able to quit any job immediately without the slightest financial concern. You will become entirely relaxed at work, knowing that you don't have to put up with any nonsense at all. Sick of your job? Quit and find another one. Financial freedom, at the very least, means freedom from fear of poverty or dependence on others. It means the ability to work as you choose, not as you need.

Some call this 'f*** you money'. The originator of the term is lost in the mists of time, but it has been popularized by John Goodman[1] and George Carlin, among others. The link at that endnote is obviously NSFW due to cussing. Be careful, you don't have that f*** you money saved, yet.

The meaning of the term is clear: if you no longer like a job, or a location, or a client, or whatever, you can use your savings to say 'f*** you' and walk away.

Being able to say 'f*** you' is an essential aspect of financial freedom. Even if you never need to do it, you *could*, and you know that you could.

Do you worry about losing your job?

Imagine that tomorrow you turn up to work only to be met at the door by a security guard who informs you that your position has been restructured and that you are to leave immediately. He accompanies you to your desk and supervises as you clear out your things, then he escorts you from the building. You try to wave goodbye to that receptionist and make a phone call gesture but she's been told not to talk to you. You find yourself on the street, shivering in the cold wind as your numb fingers struggle to keep their grip on your box of photo frames and novelty coffee mugs.

How are you feeling at this point? Are you worrying about making next month's rent? Are you concerned about missing debt repayments and getting into serious financial strife? It must be terrible living with such stress accompanying you every moment of every day. After all, in the modern economic environment, any day at work might be your last. This book will show you how to get your finances in order so that you no longer need to worry about a little thing like losing your job.

Some claim that the best way to minimize this risk is to make yourself indispensable at work. That's a great idea. However, this book is aimed at ordinary people who corporations view as interchangeable and disposable, and who lack options for immediately upgrading from that situation. This group, unfortunately, includes the greater part of the world's population. While businesses might see you as expendable, you must never see yourself that way. This book will show you how to give your life the financial dignity that it deserves.

If your finances are such that you'd easily be able to survive for a whole year, with no worries about unpayable debts, a mortgage, expenses or anything else, then you are free. You don't need to worry about losing your job anymore. While others are running around like headless chickens upon rumors of looming layoffs, your Zen-like calm will bewilder your less financially-savvy fellows. Instead of racking your brains to figure out how you'll make rent next

Wednesday if the worst comes to the worst, you'll be pondering whether to lounge on a beach in the Dominican Republic or Vietnam.

Decisions, decisions. That is financial freedom.

Could you afford sudden, major medical expenses, car repairs or legal fees?

Life is full of surprises. Not always good ones. I cannot see the future, but I can guarantee you, based on the grim laws of probability, that you will someday face a financial emergency. Everybody does at some point, and most people do so regularly throughout their lives.

Out of the blue, you might need expensive medical treatment. It happens. You probably know someone who was hale and hearty one day and undergoing emergency surgery the next. Even if you live in a country with a public healthcare system, could you afford to be out of work for six months or more? Could you manage the out-of-pocket expenses?

Most people have cars, and cars break down eventually. What would happen if you suddenly needed $1,500 for repairs, plus taxi costs while you wait? Could you handle it, or does every little funny noise from under the hood give you a minor heart attack? Careful now – medical expenses are even more expensive than car repairs.

What would happen if you were accused of a crime you did not commit, or were sued over some ridiculous matter that was not your fault? Do you have a few thousand dollars lying around to cover legal fees? Representation is essential, and expensive. It is not just for criminals, politicians and dodgy businessmen. Ordinary people can suffer legal problems too, and it can cost a bomb to get the issue fairly resolved.

This book will show you how to prepare for these life hazards. Not only will you be ready when they come; you'll also enjoy peace of mind because you'll know that if the unthinkable happens, you've got a plan and the means to put it into action.

Financial freedom means not needing to worry about how you'd pay for sudden car repairs, hospitalizations, or emergency trips to Azerbaijan to bail your sister out of jail. You know how you would pay for any of these. Unlike others, you are free from such financial cares.

Do you worry about debt?

Are you concerned that you may be in debt for many years, or even for your whole life? Would any of the problems suggested above put you in serious trouble regarding your creditors? Do you lie awake at night wondering how, or even *if*, you'll ever get out of the hole which is your financial situation? This book will provide you with a mathematical, step-by-step guide for climbing out of debt. It includes practical advice, links to free online calculators, and details of agencies that can help you.

Financial freedom means freeing yourself from the hamster-wheel of debt repayment, forever. It means that credit-card debt is a distant memory from when you were younger, sillier, and had not read this book. The day you don't owe anybody anything, you are free.

Do you wonder grimly what your future holds?

Do you ever look at your life and think, is that all there is? Working too much, rarely getting a chance to pursue your true passions, with no alternative possible in the foreseeable future?

This book will show you how to plan your own future so that you can take charge of your life and direct it wherever you want it to go. For some this simply means removing financial stress from their lives. For others it is moving to part-time work or even early retirement. Whatever your financial goals, this book will help you to set them and reach them in a logical and realistic manner.

Financial freedom means knowing what your goals are, how you'll get there, and roughly how long it will take. People don't buy a house, pay for education upfront, take a year off to go travelling, or retire early just by chance. It is not luck. It is planning. When you can plan your own future, instead of suffering the vagaries of fortune to plan it for you, then you are free.

But won't the government look after you?

Don't bank on it.

We'll come back to social security in a moment, but first consider this:

Imagine there's a tiny island nation in the Pacific. Let's call it Bananastan. It being a very quiet place, with most people meeting their economic needs through fishing and subsistence farming, not much trade takes place. In fact, over the whole of 2019 the only goods and services paid for were: twenty-seven bananas for $1 each, and a guy who fixed two thatched roofs, with each job costing $4. That means that the total value of all the goods and services bought and sold in Bananastan for 2019 was:

$$(27 \times \$1) + (2 \times \$4) = \mathbf{\$35.00}$$

We call the total of all the goods and services sold in a country the gross domestic product, or GDP. Generally the biggest, richest countries have higher GDPs while smaller, poorer countries have lower GDPs. Little old Bananastan would be the smallest economy in the world, with its GDP of just $35.

Which might be fine, but unfortunately the government of Bananastan took out a loan from the Asian Infrastructure Investment Bank in order to build a new port. The total cost of this loan? Thirty-five dollars.

The total amount owed by a national government is called the 'national debt', so Bananastan's national debt stands at $35. Now of course, big countries can have far larger debts without that being a problem, so we usually describe the indebtedness of a country by its debt as a percentage of GDP. Both Bananastan's national debt and its GDP are $35, so its debt is currently at exactly 100% of GDP. That means, if the country could somehow use all of the money raised in its economy just to pay off its debt and nothing else, it would be able to pay off the debt in one year. Obviously the government of Bananastan cannot really tax bananas and roof-fixing at 100%, otherwise no one would bother selling bananas or fixing roofs, so it will take a lot longer than that.

For comparison, the nearby, larger island of Coconutia has a GDP of $200 and a national debt of $50 which was used to subsidize a tourist attraction called The Big Coconut. Fifty dollars is a quarter of $200, so Coconutia's national debt is only 25% of GDP.

Now that you've understood those simple examples, this real-life case will make much more sense to you: the national debt of the United States currently stands at about $22 trillion, and the US GDP is a tad under that, so US national debt is a little over 100% of GDP. It is much more like the fictional Bananastan than Coconutia.

Ouch.

But wait – there's more! The US national debt only includes money owed by the federal government. State and local governments owe another $3 trillion or so.

But wait – there's more! The US government has also promised to make various payments in the future, for pensions, Medicare, social security and all those sorts of things that you might have considered depending upon for your financial needs. Some of these are already funded, i.e. they have been budgeted for or there is a trust of money available. Some of these are unfunded, i.e. no one knows where the money is going to come from. These are called 'unfunded liabilities', and are effectively a future debt that might as well be tacked on to the national debt.

What is the total of these unfunded liabilities?

According to Forbes Magazine[2], it totals more than $200 trillion.

All up, the US government owes well over 1,000% of GDP.

Suddenly Bananastan is starting to look fiscally conservative.

Perhaps the US economy will suddenly grow, meaning a greater tax intake will solve the problem. Perhaps the government will print more money, thus pushing up inflation (more about that later). But be serious: just because it is written somewhere that you are entitled to $x, does not mean that you will actually receive $x. If the government doesn't have enough money to pay your pension or whatever it is, you might receive closer to ½$x, or ¼$x, or maybe $0.

Such sudden cuts in expected payments have often occurred in other places.

For this reason, you must be prepared to look after yourself and rely on no one else. Financial freedom is not a handy add-on to your life – it is essential for your long-term wellbeing, just like your health or your ability to obey the law.

How is the national debt situation in other countries? These figures do not include unfunded liabilities.	
Country	**Percentage of total gov. debt to GDP (IMF figures)[3]**
New Zealand	26%
Australia	42%
Canada	87%
United Kingdom	87%
United States	108%
Japan	236%

What are you going to get from this book?

This is not a get-rich-quick guide. It does not require business genius, crazy risk taking or complicated financial techniques. It is a step-by-step, layman's guide for organizing your money, getting ahead and reaching your goals.

This book is not a replacement for getting professional advice. In fact, there is a whole chapter devoted to how to find a good financial advisor and how to get the most value from that advice.

A word of caution: this book is not a genie in a bottle that, upon reading, will magically grant your wish for financial freedom. To get any benefit from the book you will need to do the hard work of actually *implementing* the steps explained. This process will probably take years, though most of that time will be spent patiently waiting for the strategies to reach fruition. There are no secret tricks or shortcuts.

Before you go any further, grab a pen and paper. Also have a calculator handy, and a device with internet connection. You'll have some things to research and figure out as we go along.

Levels of Financial Freedom

What is financial freedom? It is best defined as having the wealth to choose your own path in life instead of being flung about by the fickle waves of fortune. The further down this path you go, the more freedom you will have. After all that doom and gloom, here is a rundown of what you can look forward to:

Level 1: Freedom from Fear

Your debts are under control and you have the emergency cash to bide you over in case you lose or quit your job. You don't lie awake worrying about expensive medical needs or a car breakdown because you know you could handle it financially. For most young people, this is an excellent initial goal, and if you follow the steps in this book it is likely achievable in a couple of years. You might call Level 1 'financial security'.

Level 2: Chillax

You could take a year or two off work if you wanted to, such are your savings and investments. Rumors of layoffs at your company pass by you like a gentle summer breeze. This is like Level 1 on steroids. Most people can reach this level in 5-10 years, depending on their initial circumstances.

Level 3: Semi-Financial Independence

Your wealth has reached the point where you are able to work part time, or on and off, if you wish. You can use the rest of your time to focus on other priorities. This is a great level of freedom at any age, but it is particularly pleasant for middle-aged people who are considering easing into retirement rather than finishing work all at once. Financial stress is eliminated, and options increase – work for extra cash, or play more Fortnite? At Level 3, you get to choose.

However, just because this is a nice level of freedom for older people does not mean that you only need to start thinking about it once you hit middle age. If you want to reach this point someday then you'll need to start working towards it now, if not earlier, because it will take most people 10-20 years to achieve.

Level 4: Full Financial Independence

Your investments are at a level where you can live off them permanently (but frugally). You don't have to work anymore unless you want to, either for extra pocket money or for personal fulfillment. You'll need to reach this level eventually if you want to retire, unless you live in a country that can still afford to pay a livable old-age pension by then.

There is a big FIRE movement – Financial Independence, Retire Early. These people basically follow the steps in this book to the absolute extreme in order to escape the rat race as soon as possible. A lot of FIRE websites offer fantastic advice and I link to some in this book. However, be aware that most people who are able to retire very early, before 40 or even 30, either have quite high incomes or have no children. If you fit into either of those categories then reaching this level early is plausible. If you don't, financing a comfortable retirement by age 55 might be a more suitable goal because this level of financial freedom takes most people 30+ years to achieve.

Again, that doesn't mean you can start thinking about it 30 years hence. Rather, you need to start working through the steps in this book today if you want to retire comfortably in 30 years' time.

Level 5: Rich

You don't have to work, you live in a serviced villa in the south of France, you drive a Ferrari, and you wake up every morning by doing lines of coke off the buttocks of high-class escorts. This book will not help you to reach Level 5, but if that's your goal, the best of luck to you.

Overview

Here are the steps described in each chapter and a brief summary of what to expect. The steps are arranged in a very logical order, so use this outline as an opportunity to decide where you're at and start from there.

For example, if you have trouble with debt, definitely start from the very beginning. If you have no debt and are unlikely to borrow for anything, consider starting from *Step 2: Make a Frugal Budget.*

Following the steps out of order is likely to be counter-productive. For example, you should not be making long-term investments as per *Step 8: Invest Wisely* if you don't have your emergency fund sorted out yet as per *Step 3*. If something came up, you might have to sell those investments at a loss in order to cover a short-term expense. Similarly, if you go to a financial planner as per *Step 9: Get Advice* before you've read *Step 8*: *Invest Wisely*, you will not have the investing knowledge to evaluate the advice you're getting and are more likely to end up with expensive, poorly performing financial products.

By all means read ahead, but carry out the steps in the order that they are presented. Each step builds on those before.

Finally, make sure that you read *Step 9: Get Advice* before making any big investment decisions or commitments. An advisor will help you consider whether your plan suits your individual circumstances.

Oh and remember, that there's a handy glossary at the end of this book in case you forget the meaning of terms as we go along.

With that said, here is a guide to the upcoming chapters:

Step 1: Don't Get Into (More) Debt

This chapter warns you about debt.

The main reason people lack financial freedom is that they live beyond their means, and debt is the sign of it. Avoiding new debt is so urgent that this chapter comes right at the front of the book. It outlines common debt pitfalls and how to avoid them. It also examines potentially rational reasons for borrowing money, and will offer suggestions on weighing your options and minimizing borrowing costs, together with stern and emphatic cautions.

Step 2: Make a Frugal Budget

This chapter explains how to organize and take control of your income and spending. You'll learn how to identify efficiencies in order to live within your means and to more quickly save up an emergency fund, pay back your debts, and then start saving up capital for investment.

You must NOT skip this step unless you already have a budget, and even then you'll probably find the chapter useful for all the extra tips and links that are included. A budget is essential for reaching financial freedom, and later chapters will frequently refer back to the budget that you were supposed to have made at this point.

Step 3: Establish an Emergency Fund

Yup, this is your f*** you money. Completing *Step 3* will reduce or eliminate some of those financial stressors that keep you awake at night and prevent you from realizing financial freedom. The chapter will explain why you need an emergency fund as part of your overall plan, how much it should be, and where to save it. I know I keep repeating but this cannot be said enough: *do not skip this step!* An emergency fund is the thing that will help you to avoid slipping into debt or compromising your other financial goals if and when the poo hits the fan.

Step 4: Get out of debt

This chapter details how to quickly pay off the debts you already have, and explains why doing so is vital to achieving financial freedom.

The chapter shows you how to organize your debts, figure out which ones to pay off first, and calculate how long it will take. The chapter also shows you how to get advice or plead for concessions if you've really gotten yourself into a pickle – help is available.

People who have a lot of debt are often tempted not to calculate how much of it they actually have, how much it is costing them, or how long it will take to pay off. This is natural. However, do *not* skip this step if you are so inclined. This chapter will be the toughest for a lot of readers, but also the most rewarding. Read it carefully and do what needs to be done – it will improve your financial position greatly and you will be very glad that you bit the bullet. I promise.

Step 5: Increase Your Income

This chapter is not a dodgy scheme for making a fortune. Rather, it invites you to examine your income and see if there are any practical steps you could take to earn a bit more. It contains suggestions you may not have considered.

This step is not the keystone of the whole project. As promised in the title, this book is a guide for those on low or medium incomes to build their wealth. Even if you cannot greatly increase your income, just as long as you have a reasonable surplus each month then financial freedom is within your reach. However, any increase in income will help to grease the wheels – *if* you know what to do with the extra money.

Step 6: Protect What You've Got

By this stage you've hopefully got a little wealth together. Now that you have something to lose, make sure you don't lose it! This chapter examines what types of insurance you may or may not need, plus other tips for minimizing financial risks.

Step 7: Plan Your Life

This chapter moves beyond simply avoiding financial disaster and instead focuses on your dreams and how to achieve them. These will be different for each reader. For some it might be getting out of the rat race altogether. For others, it might be a sea change to a lower-paying but more fulfilling career. Whatever your goals, you'll learn how to get there.

The chapter will show you how to use online calculators to figure out the time it will take to achieve your dreams and to spotlight ways of getting there faster. This step is very much where dreams crash into reality. Be prepared to modify your goals if they turn out to be unfeasible, but also don't be surprised if you discover that the next level of financial freedom is much closer than you had dared to hope.

Step 8: Invest Wisely

You'd think this would be an immense and complicated chapter. After all, many tomes have been written on the subject. And actually, it is the longest chapter in the book. But this step is not so immense nor so complicated that the average person cannot grasp it. We leave technical wizardry to the Warren Buffett-type geniuses and instead focus on the Everyman, bare building blocks of good investing. The reason is simple – the best investment tools for the Average Joe are straightforward and well established. Trying to get the maximum possible return through convoluted means is less productive than simply making regular investments and managing risk to a level appropriate for your needs.

You don't need to be a Brainiac to invest for financial freedom. You just need tenacity, patience and occasionally, steady nerves. This stage should be relatively easy and painless if you've already completed those earlier steps.

Step 9: Get Advice

Once you've got the basics under control and know roughly where you want to go and how you might get there in order to reach financial freedom, it's time to talk to a professional financial advisor.

Your advisor will be able to look over your plan and ensure it meets your individual needs.

Why not skip this book and go straight to the advisor? Well, finding *good* advice is hard, and getting poor to middling advice is more common than it should be. This chapter will explain how to find a suitable advisor, what questions to ask, and most importantly, what to watch out for. The lessons you learned in the earlier chapters, especially *Step 8*, will help a lot in evaluating potential advisors and making sure you find the right person (or robot, as you will see).

Step 10: Record and Reevaluate

You'll need to keep track of where your money is in order to see how things are going. Data is power. This chapter will first explain some simple ways of doing so.

Once your investments are in place and recorded, it's a matter of sticking to the plan and letting your strategy run its course. But wait! What if things change along the way, altering the financial goals that you set earlier? What if your girlfriend gets pregnant? What if you get a much higher paying job? What if you plain old change your mind and decide that your priorities have shifted? Perhaps you're no longer comfortable with having such volatile investments and would like to shift to safer ones. Maybe you decide you'll need more money in retirement due to a sudden increase in windsurfing expenses.

Everything is transient – even, sometimes, our goals. This step will explain how often you should revise your plan, and how to do so. The good news is that readjusting your plans once you're at this stage is much, much easier than starting from scratch. The hard work is done – once you get this far it's mostly fine-tuning in order to reach financial freedom.

Conclusion

In this chapter I'll congratulate you on your progress, review what we've covered, and suggest some further reading. I really hope you get this far – not only in the book, but in your actions – because I *want* you to succeed. I want you to look back some years from now at what you've achieved and think: Wow! I did it. That's what this book is all about.

A Warning

You might be thinking, meh, I'm going to move up in my career soon enough anyway. Once I'm earning the big bucks I'll pay off my debts, start investing, and all of that sort of thing. What's the point of struggling through all this now when I don't have much money anyway? It'll be easier to do it later on.

This is the path to hell.

Time is money, as will become increasingly apparent the more you read. The longer it takes to pay off your debts, the larger they will grow. The later you wait to save an emergency fund, the longer you will spend at risk of getting into a serious pickle. And the longer you put off investing, the lower your eventual returns will be.

To state this in the positive, the sooner you start working on getting your financial affairs in order, the faster you'll pay off your debts, the sooner you'll have a good safety net, and the larger your investments will grow. The time to start is today, and three years ago would have been even better.

Further, financial freedom and a high income are *not the same thing*. This is a point which will be reiterated throughout the book, to the point that you're going to get a bit tired of it. Many people with high incomes, as you will see, lack financial freedom because they have a debt-driven lifestyle, no emergency fund, and no sensible, long-term investments. On the other hand, many of those with lower incomes manage to live within their means, save, invest, and live a much more financially secure life.

That is financial freedom.

You may indeed earn a higher income one day. Good for you. Once you've read this book and followed through the steps required, that extra money will help you to reach all your goals much faster. On the other hand, if you have not learned the lessons in this book, that extra income will disappear like a sidewalk puddle on a summer's day and you will continue to experience financial distress. You'll still live beyond your means because expenses tend to rise with income. You'll risk being wiped out because you lack an emergency fund.

You may lose everything if you don't understand the fundamentals of investing.

A high income without financial know-how is like a V8 engine in a car with bald tires.

Don't believe me? Consider the case of Michael Jackson. He earned an income we can only dream of, but he died $400 million in debt. Mike Tyson earned that much over his career, but by 2003 he was in serious debt to all sorts of people. He is reportedly now solvent again. Other rich, famous people who have had to declare bankruptcy include actors Stephen Baldwin, Burt Reynolds, Gary Coleman and Kim Basinger; musicians 50 Cent, Marvin Gaye, Meatloaf and MC Hammer; and US President Ulysses S. Grant.[4]

You want one more? I can give you one more. Consider the great novelist Mark Twain. He wanted to be rich throughout his career, and he made a fortune several times over, but each time he managed to lose it through one bad investment or another.[5]

Do not wait until you have a higher income to try to reach financial freedom. Start now. By all means, attempt to increase your income as per *Step 5*, but you must also complete the other steps, in order. Vastly richer and more talented people than you and I have tried, and failed, to manage their finances through a high income alone. It doesn't work. So long as you earn enough to meet your present expenses plus a bit left over, you can reach a higher level of financial freedom than all of those celebrities managed on an enormous income.

W-wait a Minute!

Hang on, my reader yells. What makes you such an expert and why should I trust you? Are you some rich guy working in finance who will try to convince me to invest in his dodgy products? Are you someone with a high income who doesn't know what it's like to loiter in the supermarket of an evening, waiting for the staff to put discount stickers on the soon-to-expire meat? Why should I believe a word you say?

All excellent questions. I do not work in finance, nor do I have qualifications in that area. I am not a banker or a stockbroker or a financial advisor. I am a guy like you who waits for the discount stickers on the meat, and whose income has always ranged from low to medium.

How did I end up writing a book about personal finance?

One evening, exhausted after a particularly rough day at work, I searched 'early retirement' online. I found articles that said that it was mathematically possible and this began an obsessive, two-year period of intensive research and experimentation in saving and investing strategies. I've read pretty much every view on the topic (the good, the useless and the horrid), and I've made mistakes along the way.

Finally, after about a decade, I have just about realized my financial goals. I am semi-retired at age forty. I first tried retiring completely, but decided that (a) I would prefer to have a bit more spending money, and (b) I'm not ready to leave the structure of a regular job yet, so I continue to take on easy and stress-free employment as I choose.

Disclosure: it only took me ten years because I'd already repaid my student loans and had almost $100,000 saved when I started. I also lucked out with stock market returns. Lower levels of financial freedom can be achieved quickly, but reaching the higher levels takes most people much longer than a decade.

I must reiterate, I have done this on a modest income. My annual salary has hovered around $40,000, sometimes less. I got a late start in the working world and had some debts when I began, so my situation is not unlike that of my intended audience.

There are no secrets in this book. Everything here is what you could find out for free if you trawled the internet and pored over published research, and then learned from your errors and realized what is good information and what is misleading dross.

This book aims to be what I wish I had back when I started my journey about a decade ago: a concise, cogent and comprehensible summary of the information already available, with the filler, scams and time-wasters removed. I tell you what you need to know, who you need to talk to, what you need to do, and how to do it. This book is nothing more, and nothing less, than that.

I'm assuming you want the bottom line – an instruction manual for getting from Point A to Point B. Point A being your current situation and Point B being financial freedom. That's exactly what you're going to get – plus some anecdotes, vitriol, and a few lame gags along the way.

Let's start.

Who is this book for?

This book is aimed at young men with a low to medium income and little knowledge of how to manage their personal finances. If you are struggling with debt, don't know where all your money is going, or have no idea what to do with your money in general, this book is for you.

If you are in your forties already, this book will be less useful as some of the strategies take time, but by following these steps you should still be able to improve your level of financial freedom.

This book is not for those nearing retirement. In that situation, different strategies are required for managing your finances. If this is you, perhaps you might pass this book on to a nephew who might desperately need it.

If you are already well in control of your finances, have a budget, an emergency fund, and are invested in well-diversified and low-fee products, then this book is *not* for you. Give it to that beloved cousin of yours who is hopeless with money, instead.

Step 1: Don't Get Into (More) Debt

. . . and in a word, [a wise man] watches himself as if he were an
enemy and lying in ambush.

- Epictetus

Stop living on credit. Take on no more debt. Purchase only what you can afford with the money you have.

Debt and living beyond one's means are by far the biggest causes of people's financial distress. Living on credit is like running on a treadmill, regardless of your income. You run and run, working hard and paying monthly interest, sweating like a bush pig, but you never get anywhere. Unlike at the gym, you don't even derive any benefit from the exercise. If you seriously want to get off the treadmill and start moving towards financial freedom, you MUST stop living beyond your means.

There is no other way.

This is a short but essential chapter because there's no point reading about how to budget, save an emergency fund, or even how to get out of debt if you're still taking on new debt. As a wise man once said, if you find you've dug yourself into a hole, the first thing you need to do is to *stop digging.*

If you have a debt problem, it is likely that you are the kind of person who is better off not borrowing money at all, for almost any reason. Is that you? Be honest with yourself. If you are your own worst enemy when it comes to getting into debt, very seriously consider cutting up every last credit card you own.

Yes, I said it. Cut up the cards and never get another one, for the rest of your life.

Most people throughout history have survived without credit cards. You will, too. Lenders want to make them seem essential, but they are not.

You do not need a credit card.

It is true that credit cards have some advantages such as convenience and rewards for those who use them carefully – paying off the monthly balance within the no-interest period and building up a good credit score. If you are battling debt, you are probably not such a careful person. Do yourself a favor and dump the lot of them.

Get yourself a debit card instead. You can use it in exactly the same way as a credit card for store and online purchases, but it takes money straight out of your own bank account. No borrowing required. They are most commonly offered by Visa or Mastercard through banks, although there are other players in the market.

Not many people get direct mail or cold calls offering debit cards as the returns on these products for providers are much less lucrative than for credit cards. You might have to go looking.

From now on, only buy things up front. There is no need to borrow for consumer purchases if only you have a little patience. Is your car a bomb? Start saving up for a new one. If it takes two years, fine – drive (or push) the lemon for another two years. Is your washing machine broken beyond all repair? Wash your clothes in a bucket until you can afford a new one. Your great-grandma did this and so can you. Somali pirates have kidnapped your brother and they'll cut his eyes out unless you pay a heavy ransom in 48 hours? Tell him he won't have to worry about misplacing his glasses any more. If you can't afford something right now, *do without*.

Does your bank account offer some form of overdraft, i.e. allow transactions when you have insufficient funds available? Ask the bank if they can remove that facility, or see if you can do it yourself online. Do friendly people often get in touch offering you credit cards and loans and special deals? They may be doing that because clever algorithms have identified you as one of those highly profitable customers who only pays off the minimum and who ends up turning a harmless little $200 loan into a $500 return in the long, long run.

As Nancy Reagan might chide, 'just say no'.

According to the Wall Street Journal, there are people these days who use installment plans and similar to buy everyday items like sweaters, trainers and shirts, paying them off over several months.[6] One person interviewed said, "I'm not making a whole lot of money, so this is really helpful."

No, it is not helpful. If you can't afford to pay for that shirt right now, you can't afford it at all. Reduce your spending. These schemes are trying to make you buy things you can't afford in order to profit from the interest rates.

Sometimes there is no interest, but even there they are profiting by tempting you to buy things you wouldn't otherwise purchase right away. If there's no interest, you're still buying more than you can afford at the moment, which is too much. A plan of four monthly payments of $25 each sounds a lot less than $100 up front, but if you do some cunning arithmetic you'll find that actually they are equal. These options are not designed to make it easier for you to pay. They are to make it easier for you to spend unwisely.

Future You will suffer for what Present You does, just as Present You is currently on the treadmill trying to pay off all the debts and put-off expenses that Past You racked up. Do Future You a favor and avoid such payment plans altogether. Save up or do without the item. Future You will thank you. No one has ever said, "I wish I got into a whole lot more debt when I was younger."

And yet, there are a few reasons why you *might* reasonably take out a loan. We'll go through some right after this community service announcement about the scourge of STDs.

Avoid STDs – Sexually Transmitted Debts

Did you know you can catch a debt from another person? Usually it is from someone very close: your girlfriend or wife. In general, debts owed by your spouse or common-law partner are effectively also owed by you. STDs are most commonly transmitted by a partner being seduced or tricked into taking on responsibility for debts. About half the time, this is credit card debt.[7] According to one survey, about 16% of Americans have a sexually transmitted debt.[8] The survey suggests that women are slightly more likely to contract an STD than men, but men get lumped with about twice the total amount.

Here are some tips to avoid catching an STD:

1. Be wary of getting into a serious relationship with someone who is in a lot of debt. Credit card debt, auto loans and student debts are the biggest red flags to watch out for.

2. Also be wary of being with a partner who is less wise with money than you will be by the time you've finished this book. It's no good turning yourself into a financial guru only to have a partner who throws cash around like confetti.

3. Further, avoid partners who might be prone to drug or gambling addictions. These are common causes of STDs.

4. Further still, avoid partners who have other behaviors that might rack up an unpayable bill: a penchant for insanely risky investments, financially dishonest behavior, or being slack in filing tax.

5. Sometimes people need a guarantor for a loan. This is a person who promises to pay the debt if the other can't. Be very careful about signing up as a guarantor because if things turn sour you *will* be on the hook. Sometimes people are tricked by being told they are just signing as a witness. Carefully read everything before signing, and if your loved one is becoming testy about your apparent mistrust, slow down and read even more carefully.

6. If you share a credit card, you are liable for the other person's bills if they can't pay them. Sharing a card is a huge step that you should be cautious about.

7. Buying a house together is also a massive step. If the other person can't or won't pay their share of the mortgage, it's all on you. Your partner might also take out additional loans using the property as collateral, and if they lose the house, you lose it, too.

8. Be cautious about opening joint bank accounts, signing up to common phone plans, or even moving into a rental property together. All these steps have financial implications.

9. Talk openly with your girl about financial matters *long before* you consider any of the above.

10. Even if you are happily married, always keep a bit of money in your own account.

11. If your girl is not honest about any such financial matters, then you're taking a huge risk. If she has ever fibbed to you about the size of her credit card debt, imagine what else she might be hiding. Trust is essential.

12. Once things are getting serious, openly ask her to sit down together to organize finances. If she's not ready to show you all her accounts, debts, and other financial affairs, you are not ready to get serious.

14. Even once you are all settled and comfortable, keep any car registered in the name of the person who is financially responsible for the vehicle or the loan.

15. An ailment related to an STD is loaning your partner money, and then she disappears. Watch out for that one.

16. Seek professional advice about these matters before proceeding. *Step 9* will show you how to find a good advisor.

Unfortunately, there are unscrupulous people in this world, and some of them are disarmingly attractive. For such people, the easiest solution to an unpayable debt is to marry someone who is better with money, like you. Be aware that cohabitating can put you in the same legal territory as marriage. A little more about this later.

There are two final points you need to understand. First, you aren't on the hook for half of a joint debt – you are on the hook for *all* of it. Second, even if you break up or divorce, those debts will still be yours.

None of this is to discourage you from ever having joint accounts, properties and so on. This is perfectly normal for families, and it would be weird not to. Rather, this box warns you to be very careful about who you get attached to, because you'll also be attached to her debts.

Good Debts and Bad Debts

If you are borrowing to spend on something with no lasting value – a new car, a vacation, or a big night out – that is a bad debt. If you are borrowing to invest in something that may offer you a long-term financial reward – a home, a business, or skills – then it may qualify as a good investment, one that is rational to take out on your path to financial freedom.

But how can you tell which is which?

Student Debt

It can make sense to go into debt in order to study *if* this will increase your income in the long run by an amount significantly greater than the debt incurred, including interest calculated over the total period of the loan. You can use this tool to figure it out:

www.bankrate.com/calculators/managing-debt/annual-percentage-rate-calculator.aspx

Carefully calculate whether the course offers a reasonable return on investment. Weigh it up against worthy alternatives, i.e. apprenticeships, trade skills or other qualifications. If it seems like it would offer a reasonable return in an area of strong employment, proceed with caution.

You may have been told that a college degree is the path to riches, love, family, security and glory.

This is no longer the case.

Previously, only a small percentage of people had a degree, which made it stand out. These days, up to 50% of people in some countries go to university, which means you may now need a degree just to work in a post office, while a more prestigious job may require a master's or higher. As a result, some in-demand trades now offer higher average salaries than those obtained by people with less sought-after degrees.

When calculating the benefits of student debt vs future income, keep in mind that if a chosen profession might offer an annual salary of around $80,000, that does not mean you are $80,000 ahead per year. If without the qualification you could make $50,000 per year, the total return on investment is only $30,000 per year.

Actually, it is less than that. If you have to spend four years without working full time in order to get the degree, you are also missing out on that money you could have been earning, plus the returns from four years of investing your savings.

Unless you think your proposed course will leave you way ahead, be wary.

Look around for a less expensive school, i.e. a local state university or community college. Are you eligible for any scholarships? Is there a cheap online equivalent? Also, try to pay as much upfront as you can. Shop around for the best deal on a student loan you can find. Talk it through with somebody before taking the plunge. Be aware that your own parents might not be experts in this matter, because they grew up in a very different time. And make sure you finish the bloody course or else you'll be left with a debt and nothing to show for it.

There are careers counselors and others who will tell you to 'follow your passions' and 'pursue your dreams'. Well, that's fine – up to a point. Those who get into $100,000 of debt to become unemployable intersectional feminist dance therapists may find that their dream has turned into a nightmare. Is your dream or passion feasible? Do the math first. And by the way, do you think that your career counsellor's dream, when she was seventeen years old, was to one day become a career counsellor? Probably not. More likely she completed a useless degree, found she was not very employable, and ended up as a career counsellor because hey, it's a job.

I know two such cases personally.

Of course, life is not all about money and careers. We also pursue education in order to broaden our minds and exercise our curiosity about the world. But how much is that worth? Is it really better to rack up a debt of $100,000 before you've even started your working life, than to simply read a bunch of books? Your choice.

A middle path might be to take a double-degree or extra subjects outside your specialization. If you are studying electrical engineering and are also taking a class on film history, I reckon that's fair enough.

As we will see in *Step 4: Get Out of Debt*, student debts have gotten completely out of control in the US, and the situation is often described as a bubble. Some of these debts cannot even be released under normal bankruptcy laws as other debts would. Be especially careful if you study there, or anywhere else where your student debt would end up being very high. I recommend reading Aaron Clarey's *Worthless* for more information about the dangers of accruing huge debts for useless degrees, and for which fields of study might be worth your time.[9]

Property

Buying a house makes sense for some people in some circumstances. It can be a good debt in that it is a form of investment, which we'll get to in *Step 8: Invest Wisely*. Here, however, we're just talking about buying a machine for keeping the rain off yourself and your Pokémon collection.

Borrowing to buy a house makes much more sense than borrowing for a car because a car will rapidly depreciate in value whereas a house will hopefully increase in value over time. Note that this is not guaranteed. Proceed with caution.

Some people end up out of their depth with an onerous mortgage that consumes their lives and their future, and a few end up emotionally devastated if they cannot make the repayments and are forced to sell. Consider getting a smaller house in a less expensive location to minimize borrowing. Try to pay it off as quickly as possible. We will reiterate these matters in much more detail during the property section of the chapter on investments.

Start-up

Borrowing to establish or expand your own business might be a wise investment. I cannot give you specific advice for your business – you know it better than I do – but here are some things to think about.

Would it be possible to start off without borrowing, by saving up cash first? Would it be possible to borrow less, say, by starting out small-scale, on a shoestring budget? If the business starts working out and you are making a profit, you might then reinvest those returns in order to expand, instead of borrowing. See what you can do.

Essential Items

Sometimes you really need a consumer item straight away for employment or life in general, before you have time to save up for it. Such items might include a car (if your workplace is out of bicycle range and public transport is impractical), a suit, a phone, or a computer.

In such a case, borrow as little as possible. Pay as much from your own savings as you can. Don't get an awesome car – you can't afford it. The fact that someone would happily lend you the money does not change that fact. Get a secondhand car, the cheapest you can find without compromising on reliability. Tell the ladies you bought it because it belonged to James Dean before he was famous. Yup, he drove a Kia. Few know this.

As for other items essential for work, borrow as little as possible. Look for the cheapest phone that will do the job. Same for computers. There are inexpensive brands that are not great, but kind of work. Think Asus.[10]

I wonder if Asus is going to offer me a sponsorship deal after that effusive praise.

Need a suit for an interview? Check out discount or second-hand stores. Target is not your enemy.

Don't kid yourself about whether you really need the item or not. Do you have an old, dorky car that still runs? You do not need a new one. Do you have an eight-year-old laptop that still has *just* enough memory to allow software upgrades? Don't buy a new one until this one dies completely. The same goes for your phone.

Getting a Good Credit Score

Some people will tell you it makes sense to use credit cards and to pay off the balance in the interest-free period because this is inexpensive or free, and raises your credit score. This is good advice.

For *some people.*

If you can handle the discipline of using a credit card in this way, and if you plan to borrow money for some sensible reason in the future, i.e. a house to live in, this might be a rational plan. It would reduce your overall borrowing costs, which is good.

If you doubt your ability to handle a credit card in this way, or if you have no intention of borrowing in the future, I would suggest that you forgo the temptation.

You do *not need* a credit card. I am forty years old and have never owned one. There are other freaks around like me – in fact, almost a third of US households don't use one.[11] For those with a tendency to get into trouble with debt, cutting up the credit cards and using only a debit card might be the best move you can make.

Pawning

Pawn shops used to be everywhere, and you can still find them around today. The idea is, you take a valuable item to a pawn shop, say, your great-aunt Maggie's engagement ring, and borrow money using it as collateral. Then you repay the money upon the agreed date, with interest, and the pawn shop gives you the ring back.

If you can't repay the loan, they keep the ring.

If you are desperate for cash, pawning an item might actually be a better idea than getting into credit card debt, taking out a pay day loan, or going to a loan shark named Tony 'The Bulgarian'.

The reason is, if you can't pay the loan, the shop takes the item and you are free and clear, with no remaining debt accruing ever larger and more intimidating levels of compounding interest. Remember, it is an option. And also remember, simply selling something you own for quick cash is better yet.

Final Thoughts

In Western countries it has become normal and accepted to borrow money for all sorts of things. It has become so ingrained that people rarely question it.

Question it.

It is possible to get through life without borrowing a *cent*. A century ago, ordinary people often did not borrow money at all, especially for consumer items. Those who did take out loans usually needed them to buy a house, a farm, or materials for their business. Consumer credit only became commonly available with growing wealth. Funny, isn't it – you'd think as people become richer they'd feel less need to borrow money, but the opposite is the case.

Just because you are *able* to buy something now and pay it back later with interest doesn't mean that you *should* do so. Avoid consumer debt, i.e. fun stuff that will not make you any money. If you cannot resist, there is no point reading this book any further because Steps 2-10 assume that you've already broken the habit. If you must borrow for some sensible investment such as those listed above, do so as though you are cat-sitting a Bengal tiger – very, very carefully.

Step 2: Make a Frugal Budget

If you set a high value on liberty, you must set a low value on everything else.

\- Seneca

Hopefully you have been persuaded to avoid taking on any more debt, and you are now ready to 'dig up' instead of just 'stop digging'. It's almost time to make some real progress towards your financial freedom by saving and paying off any existing debts.

But you might still be wondering, how do financially secure people manage to live without credit, even if their income is similar to, or lower than, your own? How are they able to get to the end of each month with no debt, and even with some savings to add to the pile? Is there some trick to this that I need to know?

There *is* a trick to doing this, and you do need to know it.

The strategy is a brilliant, highly classified piece of financial wizardry. It is like the most awesome kung fu move you ever saw, where Bruce Lee flicks a giant, scary, boulder of a man with his little finger, sends him flying across the room, knocking over dozens of other villains, before finally crashing into a cabinet full of delicate glassware.

This secret of wealth and comfort was found hidden in ancient scrolls that had been stowed in a remote cave near the shores of the Dead Sea. Normally you'd have to attend an expensive, week-long workshop in order to access this profound knowledge, but today I'm offering it to you for no more than the cover price of this book.

Ready?

This ancient, mystical wisdom is . . .

Spend less than you earn.

Just as eating more calories than you burn makes you fat, and eating less than you burn makes you skinny, the same happens with money. Here is the formula:

Spending > Income = Debt

Spending < Income = Savings

It continues to astonish me how many people fail to grasp this basic mathematical truth.

To paraphrase the famous Charles Dickens quote, happiness is an annual income of $30,000 and annual expenses of $29,999. Misery is an annual income of $30,000 and expenses of $30,001.

There are three ways to approach this formula. You can increase your income, decrease your spending, or both. This chapter will focus on the spending side of the equation, and *Step 5* will focus on income.

The greater the gap between your income and spending (in the right direction), the more your financial freedom will increase. To expand the gap, you'll need to figure out exactly where your money is going and look for areas to adjust. You need to make the invisible hole, visible.

You need to make a budget.

Only about a third of Americans have a household budget,[12] and this figure is likely similar in the other Anglophone countries. Those with higher than average salaries are most likely to budget. However, everyone needs to make a budget, however simple, in order to manage expenses and start nearing financial freedom.

There are two ways of starting a budget. The first is simply to record everything you spend for a month while remembering to factor in less frequent expenses such as car registration and Christmas shopping. You might do this by hand, or set up your own spreadsheet. Keep your receipts and check your bank statements to help you do this.

The second, easier method is to use a budgeting app to do much the same thing in more detail and with some built-in charts and calculators. There are many, many of these apps, and a lot of them are excellent. You can keep your phone with you and note down each transaction as you make it.

Two common and useful ones worth mentioning are Mint[13] and YNAB.[14] There are so many available that I could not possibly research them all – have a look around and find the one that best suits your needs. Some are purely budget apps, while others also help you to keep track of debts, investments, savings and so on – decide whether you want a simple one or a really detailed one. A simple one is fine for now but later on, when we're looking at how to manage your investments, you might want to upgrade to a fancier one.

Writing down every single expense is a hassle so I highly recommend you use an app to save time, and also for the automatic statistics it can generate to quickly figure out where all your money is disappearing to. Why not? We live in the future!

Most of these apps have a free and a paid version. Try the free version first, and if the program suits you, consider shelling out. This would be a perfectly sound investment of your money.

Crazy as it may seem, the trick to getting value from these apps is to actually *use* them. You can download as many as you like, but unless you're actually recording each transaction as you make it, you will get no benefit from it whatsoever. It would be like buying a home gym and then letting it gather cobwebs, wondering the whole while why your arms still look like noodles and your potbelly is unchanged. While apps have many advantages over pen and paper versions, or your own spreadsheet, there's no point having any of them unless you're going to regularly record your spending.

If you do use a budget app or equivalent diligently, after a few months you will have generated some powerful, potentially life-changing data.

I'm going to harp on this point for a while because I know many readers are going to grumble, bah, I'll do it some other time, and will never get around to it.

What, exactly, are the advantages of a budget?

How a budget app saved me

I'd just moved to the Philippines and was trying to live independently on a certain income. Wisely, I downloaded and started using a budget app to help me keep track of my spending. I had no idea how to divide up my budget because it was a new country, so I tried to live a somewhat frugal life, recording each purchase for a month to see how things were going.

I knew I was spending too much. *Way* too much. A glance at my bank statements indicated that I was withdrawing almost twice as much money as I ought to have, over the first month or two. But where was it all going?

I suspected that I may have been spending too much on eating out. Also, I was often taking my girlfriend out to dinner, which doubled that amount. Grocery shopping seemed more expensive than it ought to be. Was I buying too much of the pricier fruit like mangoes? Or those imported goods like raisins and cashews?

I also suspected several other expenses of being the culprit that was breaking the budget: scuba diving lessons and trips, visa expenses, gym fees, phone and internet payments, and various others.

Or was it the combination of all of these? What was I to do?

Once I had a good month or so worth of data diligently entered into my app, I pressed the magic button that gave me a circle chart of my spending, and in a fraction of a second I saw my real problem:

Rent.

This one expense totaled around 40% of my total spending! The second largest expense was bills at 19%. Groceries? Only 10%, so I could go ahead and eat as many mangoes as I wanted. Eating out? 5%. The gym? 2%. Phone and internet? Point one percent!

Had I not used the budget app I may have wasted time, money and effort trying to eat out less often, looked for a cheaper gym, or inconvenienced myself with the slightly cheaper off-peak gym deal. Instead, because of the app, I saw immediately that the first thing to do was obviously to find a cheaper place to live. There was no point in finding any other savings until I had done that.

Without this information I would have had little hope of getting my budget under control and making my savings last. With it, I was able to do so within a couple of months. For me, this was the difference between financial freedom and eternal financial slavery – that simple, free app.

Upcoming chapters focus on saving an emergency fund, paying off debts, and investing. Keeping a strict budget is the key to achieving these steps on the path to financial freedom. Without a budget, you can't do it.

Even some people with very high incomes are often unable to stay out of debt or to save anything for the future because of their inability to live within their means, i.e. to *budget*. On the surface they appear rich: a beautiful house, a luxury car, expensive clothes. Scratch the surface and you'll often find a household in extreme financial distress, taking out more and more loans in order to keep up appearances. Things are not always as they appear. Remember: if you have an income of $200,000 and expenses of $210,000, you are a slave to debt. If you have an income of $30,000 and expenses of $25,000, you are much closer to financial freedom.

A high income is not the key to financial security. Living within your means is.

Lowly folk like us on low to middle incomes are sometimes able to better manage our affairs and plan ahead than some apparently wealthy people, thereby suffering fewer financial woes in the long run. That's how much difference a budget can make.

Properly fulfilling this step could directly lead to:

- Getting out of debt months or years earlier, thus saving you hundreds or thousands of dollars.

- Paying off your home several years sooner, thus saving you tens of thousands of dollars.

- Retiring years or DECADES earlier. You might only be 25 now, but trust me, one day having the option to retire at 50 instead of 65 will be huge.

Let's look at a concrete example to see how much of a difference budgeting can potentially make: Trevor is hopeless at saving because he does not keep a budget. He only manages to save $200 a month. Let's say he consistently invests this $200 in the stock market. If he started doing this in 1999, and if we assume the monthly contribution will increase with inflation, then twenty years later, in 2019, he would have total savings of $115,000.

But what if Trevor somehow read this book back in 1999, gradually sorted out a reasonable budget, and managed to put away $1,000 a month instead? Making all the same assumptions, by 2019 he would have $440,000. Quite a difference, and such improvements in savings are feasible for many people. Follow the link at the endnote to see the online calculator I used to figure out this hypothetical case.[15]

[**Edit**: Yes, Trevor's example ends just before the 2020 stock market crash, because that's when this book was written. Nevertheless, the period 1999-2019 includes two previous crashes and is therefore reasonable. Much more about shares and crashes coming up in *Step 8: Invest Wisely*.]

By sorting out his expenses, Trevor ends up with an extra $325,000 in his pocket. That is the power of budgeting.

Have I got your attention yet?

This is a time-consuming step. You might like to put this book aside for a month or so, get your budgeting app, diligently fill it with data, then come back here to see what's next. I'll be right here when you're ready to continue.

Don't try too hard to modify your spending yet. We'll demonstrate how to do that in the following section.

And by the way, I know that some of you are strongly averse to doing this because you *know* that you overspend at the pub or on whatever your weakness is, and you fear seeing the actual figure. You don't want to look. You don't want to know the awful truth. This is common and natural.

However, reaching financial freedom means using facts and figures to help you, and you *must* find out precisely what is going on, however painful it may be. The exact numbers matter. Would you go to a doctor who was too squeamish to look at your gaping wound? If you're not prepared to look at the mangled limb or flesh-eating bacteria that is your spending, you are going to be just as unable to cure what ails you.

*   *   *   *   *

Welcome back. I told you I'd be here.

Before we continue, let's look ahead: after this general discussion of how to improve and manage your budget, there is a clear, simple, and hopefully amusing example to illustrate. If something is confusing at first, keep reading a few more pages until you get to the example to see how this process works in the real world.

Now that you know where your money is going, you need to decide where it ought to be going. Make a list (perhaps with your app) of each budget area and decide how much should go into it. Divide the list into *fixed* and *discretionary* expenses.

A fixed expense is one that you cannot avoid, like grocery shopping or car repayments, though you may find ways to reduce it. A discretionary expense is one that you can choose to spend on, or not: a snakeskin car seat cover or a tour of Scottish distilleries.

For annual expenses like tax or car registration, break it up into twelve parts. Also remember to budget for upcoming, one-off expenses. If you're expected to give a $60 gift for your cousin's wedding in three months, budget this as $20 over each of those months and put it away. I find it handy to have an 'extras' category because something unexpected always comes up.

Now that you can see exactly where your money is going, it's easier to identify potential savings. Carefully consider each item and try to figure out where you could cut back. Spending a lot eating out? Cook more at home. Are supermarket expenses too high? Perhaps there's a local market or a budget chain you could use instead. Spending a lot going out and partying? Be one of those despised customers who buys one drink and sits on it all night. Whisky is good for this because beer is horrible once it gets warm.

If you're spending a lot on buying a coffee on the way to work five days a week, get up five minutes earlier and make your own. Little expenses like that can really add up: $3.50 coffee x 250 mornings a year = $875.00. Ouch. That's a lot more than buying your own mocha pot.

You might notice other expenses that could be cut down - could you live somewhere cheaper? Perhaps you could find a share house or a smaller apartment, or live in a dodgy area and carry a plank of wood with a nail through it every time you go outside.

Could you live without a car? A motorbike or scooter might be cheaper. A bicycle would be cheaper still. Could you spend less on clothes? Second-hand stores often have great, classic gear so long as you have an eclectic aesthetic (try saying that three times fast) and the patience to search. Choose items of clothing that go together in various combinations, so you need fewer clothes overall. Earth colors help here. You might feel like Scrooge, but remember, Scrooge was heaps rich.

Don't try to change everything at once. It will be too hard and you'll give up. Identify your biggest discretionary expense, modify it, then work on the next one. After all, each one is a lifestyle change and will take a while to become a habit. Normally it takes about a month to get used to any such change, so unless your financial situation is truly dire, try making one change per month, and notice how your budget gradually gets further into the black after each adjustment.

I can't tell you precisely what to do here. This is the bit where you meticulously go through all of the expenses you have so painstakingly recorded and ponder for yourself how each could be reduced or eliminated. The more parsimonious you are at this stage, the closer you will be to financial freedom.

Find out how cheaply you can live a good life and set that as your *permanent* baseline of expenditure. That word 'permanent' is essential, as we will see in the next chapter on increasing your income.

The Two Magical Budget Items

There are two expenses that you're actually going to try to *increase*, rather than decrease. These are the most important budget items of all. These expenses are the key to all future wealth creation and to reaching financial freedom. These items are, basically, the part where you are paying yourself and increasing your net worth.

Ready for them?

Savings and *paying off debt.*

All the other expenses you are trying to reduce as much as possible, but these expenses are the ones you are trying to grow. The more you can save and pay off debts (if you have any), the more capital you'll have to work with when we get up to investing. Any savings made in other budget items should be immediately transferred to savings and/or paying off debt. This is the key for turning your efforts with that budget into wealth creation and financial freedom.

Savings comes under discretionary expenses and debt comes under fixed expenses.

Save an emergency fund first, or pay off debts first?

The next chapter explains what an emergency fund is, where to save it and how large it should be. It is essentially a rainy-day fund, and you definitely need one for financial freedom. But you also need to rapidly pay off your debts in order to reach financial freedom, as will be explained in the chapter after that. Which of these should you do first?

Here is the order of operations:

1. If you have debt, first save up a small emergency fund. This should be enough to cover your expenses for about three months. For example, if you live on $2,000 a month, then you'll need to save up an initial emergency fund of $6,000.

---

2. Start aggressively paying off your debts, one by one in the order explained in *Step 4: Get Out of Debt*. Do not cut into your emergency fund to do this. That fund is, as the name suggests, only for emergencies, and you'll need to top it back up every time there is an actual emergency like car repairs or a medical bill.

3. Once all debts are completely paid off, not including a mortgage if applicable, start enlarging your emergency fund to make it as generous as I will recommend in *Step 3* (sneak peek: enough for six months to a year of expenses).

4. Once you are debt-free *and* have a 6-12 month emergency fund saved, further savings should go into your investments, as described in detail in *Step 8: Invest Wisely*. House payments might be included as an investment. Remember, no money from your emergency fund is to go into investments. That money stays right where it is, and immediately gets topped up with income earmarked for investment if it is ever depleted.

The rationale: you need an emergency fund regardless of your situation, hence it is the highest priority. Debt comes next because debts cost you money the longer you have them. Third comes increasing the emergency fund because having only three months of expenses saved is living on the edge, and you don't want to do that for any longer than necessary. Last is investing because you generally can't make long-term investments until you're out of debt and have a good emergency fund set up.

A note for homeowners or those planning to be one: sometimes it can make sense to make long-term share market investments even while you are paying off a mortgage, depending on various circumstances. This is probably more advanced than my readers are ready for at the moment so I will not get into the details, but hit the links at the endnotes for further information.[16] [17]

This order of priorities is convoluted but important. Consider bookmarking this page and referring back to it as we reach the chapters on saving an emergency fund, paying off debt and investing.

Here is an absurdly simple, example budget for one month, to give you an idea of how it works. Imagine this is your budget, that you do not yet have an emergency fund saved, and that the monthly payment on the car loan listed is the minimum allowed:

Income	$2,000

Fixed expenses

Rent	$860
Car payment	$424
Groceries	$420
Electricity	$110

Discretionary expenses

Gym membership	$46

Beer/eating out	$50
Madam Phoebe's House of Pain	$70
Savings	$20

Let's say, after reviewing your budget app, you gradually begin to identify a few savings. By turning off the lights when you leave the room you get the power bill down to $105, saving $5 (yeah not much, most of the bill is the connection cost). By cutting back on the expensive brand of baked beans and buying cheaper cuts of meat you manage to reduce the grocery bill to $390, saving $30. By cooking more at home and drinking less you reduce beer/eating out to $30, saving $20, and you decide it would be in your interests to cut out the House of Pain altogether – after all, you were only going there to support your old school friend Phoebe in getting her new business started . . . or whatever, but in any case, you save $70 there.

Let's add those savings together, in order:

$$\$5 + \$30 + \$20 + \$70 = \$125.$$

And now let's look at your new budget. Note how **100%** of this additional, surplus income has been added to savings (because you lack an emergency fund.)

Also note that **0%** of that $125 has been added to any other item, like a more expensive gym membership, nor has any been used to fund any new expenses like a pet goanna or one of those Ab machines they're forever advertising on TV. This is the most important part: reductions in spending MUST be put directly into savings at this point, otherwise you will never reach financial freedom.

Fixed expenses

Rent	$860
Car payment	$424
Groceries	$390
Electricity	$105

Discretionary expenses

Gym membership	$46
Beer/eating out	$30
Savings	**$145**

Now you're cooking with gas! Multiplying by 12, you've increased savings to $1,740 a year instead of a piddling $240 under your old budget.

In this example, once you've saved up an initial emergency fund of around $5,500 (three months of expenses), you can start putting all those extra savings straight into increasing car repayments above the minimum. Once the car is fully paid off, use savings to increase the emergency fund to $11,000-$22,000 (six to twelve months of expenses). And when *that's* done, all further savings go into savings for investments, as we will discuss in *Step 8*.

I can't tell you exactly how much you ought to be saving, except 'as much as possible'. Some advisors suggest that saving and investing around 15% of your income throughout your working life should give you a decent retirement income[18] – but you'll need to establish your emergency fund and pay off consumer debts before starting on that. The more you save, the faster you can get those tasks out of the way.

In order to retire early, you'd need to save more than 15%. Those racing to reach the upper levels of financial freedom commonly save 50% of their income – and some manage even more than that.[19]

It's up to you.

You will have noticed that in the example budget above, it would still take you several years to save up an emergency fund and pay off your debts, let alone get up to investing. The coming chapter on increasing your income may help you to push those savings higher and reach goals faster than currently seems feasible.

More handy hints for managing your money

- It might be possible to have deductions automatically taken from your salary or bank account and put into a savings account or investment, if you're ready for that. Setting this up once can help if willpower is a problem.

- Read your bank statements monthly. Are you still paying for some stupid online membership that auto-renewed without you realizing? The scoundrels *assume* you'll forget and that's how they make their money. I'm ashamed to say I've been stung by that caper more than once. Cancel it straight away. If you haven't checked your bank statements lately, there's a good chance you have two or three of these little bastards hanging around. It might only be five or ten bucks a month but it all adds up.

- Go on cheap dates that don't seem cheap. Coffee then a walk in the local park so you can point out a pair of nesting snowy egrets. Attend public events like fireworks or festivals. Day hikes. Free/cheap museums and art galleries. Better yet, date a rich, older woman who will subsidize your lifestyle. Hey, I'm kidding! Or am I?

- Enjoy inexpensive holidays: camping, staying in youth hostels, hiking, etc. I've been on week-long trips that cost little more than staying home for the week.

- You may be paying for things that you don't need. For example, I found out I was paying for life insurance through my superannuation account that was useless because it was not valid while I was overseas. After five years of paying for nothing I finally got wise and cancelled it. Go over all your financial affairs and see if there's an inefficiency that can be rectified.

- Many banks are blackguards. They flay you alive with fees at every turn. Want to make a deposit? Oh, you've got to pay them a fee for the honor of giving them your money. Want to check your bank balance at an ATM? Sometimes there's even a fee for that. See if you can get a better deal with a small bank or credit co-op.

- Never go shopping without a shopping list. If you go to the supermarket, you should already know what you're going to cook that week and the ingredients required. If clothes shopping, you should know the exact item you are after, and come home with no unexpected items. If you see something else you want – how much can you really need it, if yesterday you didn't even know it existed? Instead, ask your grandma to get you that adorable Dalek salt and pepper shaker set for Christmas. Impulse purchases are for wimps.

- If there are non-perishable food items that you regularly consume, walk down that aisle every time whether you need any or not. If it happens to be on sale, buy heaps and hoard a stash. I do this with things like tuna, sauce, oats and my favorite pasta.

- If you are considering a big purchase, it can help to put it off for a while to consider it. A few weeks from now you might decide that you don't need that expensive new jacket after all, or a good-enough one might go on sale somewhere else. At the very least, sleep on it. If you see something great while you're online or at the mall, don't buy it straight away. There are very few things that you really need NOW NOW NOW. Most things can wait. Consider how you might fit it into your budget for some time down the track.

- Relocation, Relocation, Relocation. Are you able to do the same job in a cheaper location? For example, are you able to move to the countryside, or to a less expensive city? Here's a big one to consider: are you able to work for the same salary in a cheaper country? Do some research and check it out. If you're prepared to do it, the savings are likely to dwarf those found in avoiding overpriced Starbucks coffee or using a cheaper gym.

- Alternatively, could you save money by living with family, joining a share house or taking in a boarder?

How to stick to your budget

Different people have different tricks for adhering to their budget. Some only spend in cash. For example, imagine a budget of $2,000 a month, excluding savings. One could withdraw $500 from an ATM each Monday and try to last until the next Monday until withdrawing any more.

This has several advantages. Firstly, spending cash really makes you *feel* like you're spending money. You can literally see it disappearing from your hands. Using cards, phones or making online purchases is not so visceral, and that electronic money can slip away without you even noticing it. Research suggests people will spend up to 83% more with a card,[20] because they are not feeling the pain *right now*. But they will feel it. People who have trouble controlling their spending sometimes find that going all-cash or almost all-cash (excluding bills that need to be paid online) can help.

Further, the physical limit of cash in your wallet is a constant reminder that you need to restrain your spending. If it gets to Saturday night and you only have $40 left in your pocket, you'll hopefully limit your partying so that you don't have to go hungry on Sunday.

Another handy aspect of cash is that you can put it into labeled envelopes for the month – a groceries one, a rent one, and so on. In this way you'll soon notice that one of them is getting light and see that you've overdone it.

For those who'd prefer to keep things electronic, that budgeting app you downloaded should be just as useful now as it was when you first set up your budget. Enter each purchase as you make it, and consult the program regularly to see if you're sticking to your plan. If you do this consistently it should work as well as putting cash into separate envelopes.

At first your friends will laugh at you when you're out on the town and old Tighty McTightface pulls out his phone to record every little bit of money leaving his pocket . . . but after they see how your finances improve compared to their own, and how much less stress you suffer, they'll stop laughing and start imitating you instead.

Unless they're idiots or something.

Speaking of friends, it might help if you have someone to join you on this journey. If you have a mate who's pretty good with money, tell him what you're up to and get his suggestions. You might also have a partner or relative who is financially savvy.

If you get a sudden, unexpected windfall – your great-aunt dies leaving you a small inheritance, and seven cats – what do you do?

Budget it. Use some to splurge on, and plan where the splurge shall take place. Save the rest. For example, if you come into $5,000 unexpectedly after a win at bingo, use $500 to buy that new phone you desperately want, spend another $500 on wine, women and song, and save $4000. This is much easier than trying to save all $5,000.

However, if you still have debt, the splurge shall be a $5 craft beer and all the rest will go into repayments. Debtors don't get to have as much fun as everyone else.

If you break your budget, treat it as you would missing a gym session or being late for work. Don't berate yourself – fix the problem. Think: where did I go wrong, and how shall I rectify it?

If it was because you hung out with Trevor and then, as always happens, you woke up with little recollection of what happened or where all your money went, then you'll need to be much more disciplined around him in future, or avoid him altogether. I know those guys are the most fun, but you must keep yourself from temptation if you want to reach financial freedom.

If you slipped up while browsing Amazon or similar, try to avoid those sites. You might even self-lock them on your browser and put the password somewhere difficult to reach.

Figure out why you went wrong and use the experience to do better next time.

As for the money, the ideal would be to skimp harder the following month to make up for it, but if your budget is so tight that this is impossible, so be it.

Remember, everyone who budgets screw up from time to time, and yet they are always far ahead of those who don't budget at all, just like guys who occasionally sleep in and miss the gym are still in much better shape than those who never go to the gym. Your budget will help you reach financial freedom even though you are a fallible human being. It is a spending plan, not the Ten Commandments. You don't go to Hell if you spend $30 too much on beer one weekend. If your budget is stressing you out, you're doing it wrong.

To stretch the religious theme a little further, your budget is like the Sabbath. The God of Finance made the Budget for Man, not Man for the Budget. Chill out. If you planned to save $1,000 a month but only managed $800, so be it. Other people with no budget saved nothing and instead went even further into debt. So long as you have a budget, you're on the right track.

If you're constantly breaking your budget, are you aiming too high? Perhaps you need to reduce your savings rate to a more reasonable level to ensure that you can pay the bills and keep yourself fed. Remember, most of your flexibility is in the discretionary spending – the fixed spending has to be spent, no matter what you do. Don't cut back on anything essential like veggies, soap, contraceptives . . . you can see for yourself how this will turn out to be a false economy.

Final thoughts

Continue to review your spending from time to time, especially by going over your bank statements, and look for additional savings or unnecessary costs. Check online for further advice – there are lots of minimalist lifestyle and financial independence blogs that can give you countless tips on saving money. Here are a couple that I like:

www.mrmoneymustache.com/

www.theminimalists.com

In conclusion, a small reversal. It is possible to *waste* money by being cheap. For example, don't buy a $2,000 car that will cost you thousands in repairs to keep on the road. My friend once bought a car for a case of beer. The man who got the beer got the better end of the bargain. The car engine would not start unless it was hot-wired (exposed wires were left out under the dash for this purpose), you could see the road between your feet, and the roof did not work when it started raining. He only managed to get a roadworthy certificate because his brother was a mechanic.

This car was not 'good enough'.

Don't buy cheap and nasty clothes that will soon wear out, or which you are ashamed to wear. Buy the things you need to buy, at a level of quality that will adequately do the job.

In *Step 5* we'll examine the other side of the budget equation – how to increase your income. However, we'll first take a closer look at those two magical items on your list of budget items: savings and debt payments.

Step 3: Save an Emergency Fund

The shortest period of time lies between the minute you put some money away for a rainy day and the unexpected arrival of rain.
- Jane Bryant Quinn

You're no longer living on credit and you have a budget. Nice work! It must be time to start using that lovely surplus income for paying off debt, right? Or for investment? What comes next, again?

Think about it . . .

Wouldn't it be awful if some random event came along and totally messed up your budget and forced you back into (deeper) debt? Something like a medical emergency, car repairs, losing your job for being caught reading a politically incorrect blog at work, legal fees because you get locked up in an Indonesian prison on trumped-up charges, an F-35 crashing into your house, etc. etc. Well, here's some bad news. As time passes, the probability of some such random, nasty event occurring approaches 100%. In other words, bad things *do* happen from time to time. It is not a risk. It is a certainty.

You've got to be ready.

A colleague recently needed car repairs that cost around $1,000. She complained that it was hard to scrape up the money. She had to cancel a planned trip and she ended up borrowing some of the total from her mum.

This is my colleague I'm talking about. Someone who has an income comparable to my own. Not a huge amount of money, but plenty. I wouldn't say this to her face, but if you're a gainfully employed adult who can't easily afford a random $1,000 expense that comes out of the blue, you are irresponsible. You have to be liquid enough to manage the various, minor vagaries of life. Such an expense should be annoying but not stressful. Because you ought to be prepared. This is the final step towards reaching Level 1 of Financial Freedom – freedom from fear. It is the 'f*** you' money we discussed back in the introduction, which gives you the freedom to walk away from a bad job, client or location if you've had a gutful.

To complete this step, you need to set up an emergency fund. This is an at-call, high interest bank account or money market fund with enough money in it to get you through an average-sized disaster or greater.

How Much?

How much money is enough? Back in *Step 2: Make a Frugal Budget*, I told you to put away sufficient cash for three months' living expenses before you start aggressively paying off debts. If you have debts (aside from a mortgage), this is the amount to shoot for. If you are debt-free, it is time to level-up your emergency fund: it should be enough for six months' to one year's worth of living expenses.

That's quite a range. How much is right for you? It depends on your circumstances and comfort with risk. If your career is contract to short-term contract you might need more; if you have a more stable job or are pretty Zen then you might be content with less. I personally have enough to live frugally for a year in an inexpensive country because I'm single and mobile. If you have a family then six months' worth of living expenses would be the bare minimum I would dare suggest, and I would highly recommend closer to a year's worth. Otherwise, how will you meet all your obligations, such as mortgage payments and monthly bills, if you lose your job and cannot quickly find another?

Where to Keep It

Your emergency fund should be in readily available cash, not a term deposit (also called a CD or time deposit) that is hard to withdraw without paying a large penalty.

Option 1: Money market account (MMA)

Outside the US, many different names are used. In plain English, it is a high-interest bank account. See what products your current bank offers, and check out competitors online. Ensure that you can withdraw your money at any time. This type of account sometimes limits the number of transactions allowed per month, but that's okay because you'll rarely draw from the account anyway. This is the simplest option for your emergency fund because your existing bank may have something suitable, which makes transferring money to and from your daily transactions account super easy. Some online bank accounts also offer competitive interest rates.

Option 2: Money market fund

It sounds almost the same, but this is a mutual fund that pools your money with others and invests in low-risk, low-return cash and short-term securities. Check out the options provided by Vanguard, Black Rock and others. Keep in mind that it can take a few days to withdraw your money from this account, so also maintain enough in a bank account to cover immediate emergency requirements. This option might suit you if it offers a considerably higher interest rate than a high-interest bank account. But does it? Do not assume this. Check it out first and see if it's worth the extra complication.

Look around for the best interest rate you can get for such an account. I have a 'Bonus Saver' account for this purpose that offers a higher return if you make regular deposits and no withdrawals. Once or twice a year I have to make a withdrawal because I need quick cash for something or other, and I lose that month's bonus interest rate. No biggie.

When you get up to *Step 9 – Get Advice*, you can ask your advisor for suggestions about where to put your emergency fund. If in doubt, go for a high interest bank account/MMA offered by your existing institution for the time being.

Because I live overseas I keep an additional few thousand dollars in a local bank, in the local currency, in case my Aussie bankcard is not accepted for some reason. I also have a few hundred dollars in United States dollars (cash) handy while traveling in case I can't get to an ATM for some reason. I've only needed to use this once, when none of the ATMs at Shanghai Airport would accept foreign bank cards and the hotel could not process my debit card. Sometimes everything goes wrong all at once.

It's no good having money for emergencies if you can't access it in an emergency.

By the way, I also keep a little cash in a side pocket of my day bag in case I ever forget my wallet. I also keep in there an umbrella, condoms, spare tissues, a hanky, headache medicine, band aids and a few other odds and ends whenever I go out. I'm that kind of person.

Do like the Boy Scouts with your finances: be prepared!

The Reward

Aside from the financial advantage of never needing to borrow for emergencies and thereby fall back into debt, the emergency fund gives you peace of mind. Once you have saved it up, you will no longer have a near heart attack when your car struggles to start, or when you get hit with a random tax bill you didn't see coming. You'll merely grumble, pay it, and get on with your merry life.

You'll be much more relaxed at work when you know that, if need be, you could walk away. You'll be more willing to say no to unreasonable demands, speak your mind if necessary, and filter work calls once you get home. If it came to it, you could even reject a rude customer or stand up to a bullying boss. Remember, you have f*** you money in your pocket. Any time you want, you can walk out the door.

Anecdotally, people who reach the 'position of f*** you' do not actually storm out the gates while playing the boss' head like the bongo drums. More commonly, they become bolder and more assertive; happy to work hard and do their jobs properly, but unwilling to be treated like a doormat. [21] You've probably experienced this feeling already, when you've already handed in your two weeks' notice and are starting to wrap up. You still get your tasks done, but you feel much more relaxed, and any workplace dramas are a source of comedic amusement. Having your emergency fund set up turns this tranquil period into a permanent reality.

There's always that one employee who dares to speak up for what the others are thinking. Sometimes it is because they are naturally quarrelsome, but in other cases it is because their position is very firm. Soon, that will be your position.

Replenishing the Emergency Fund

Every time you cut into your emergency fund, you must top it up again straight away, even if it means putting other financial goals on hold. If you are still paying down debt, ease off and pay only the minimum until you get your emergency fund back to three months' worth of living expenses, *then* get back to paying off those debts aggressively. Lacking an emergency fund puts you at risk of falling into further debt if a sudden expense comes up, so it must take precedence. Remember, avoiding new debt comes before paying off existing debt.

If you have no debts, pause your investing (*Step 8*) until you have your emergency fund filled back up. Remember, you should have chosen an amount that will keep you going for six months to a year. Once the emergency fund is topped up, you can get back into making those wonderful investments – but there's to be no investing until you have your financial parachute ready to go.

Let's look at the emergency fund in action with these charming examples:

Imagine that Tim has responsibly saved $9,000, which is enough for him and his young family to live on for three months. Now he is fully focused on paying off his debts, as per the next chapter.

One day Tim is hit by a truck while riding his bicycle, and receives no compensation for required medical treatment because he was foolishly using an umbrella at the time. He has to cut into his emergency fund to pay $3,000 in out-of-pocket expenses.

Tim now needs to slow down his payment of debt to the minimum permissible in order to top up his emergency fund. Once it is back up to $9,000, he can return all his financial firepower into paying down those debts. And once those are paid off, he can start making long-term investments.

Compare the case of Tom. He has no debt and has already saved up a 12-month emergency fund of $36,000. He is currently putting his surplus income into long-term investments.

Tom is a very bad driver, and one day he drives right off the road and totals his car. Insurance does not cover the damage because he admits that he was eating a sandwich, drinking coffee, reading a book and plucking his nasal hair at the time.

He needs to buy a new car, and the cheapest that will do costs $12,000. He cuts into his emergency savings account for this, not his long-term investments.

Tom then spends some months putting every cent of new savings into his emergency fund. Once it is back up to $36,000, he resumes putting money into investments.

Final Remarks

One final note - inflation means that your emergency fund should gradually increase over time. Changed circumstances might also cause you to reconsider the amount required, i.e. if there are rumors going around of layoffs at your company or if you take on a mortgage. Review the amount about once a year and adjust as required.

What, my reader asks, is that it?

Yes!

Setting up an emergency fund is super simple, but too few people actually do it. Spend a few months getting it organized and you'll be a financial brown-belt. You will have already reached Level 1 of financial freedom – freedom from fear.

How well prepared are we for financial emergencies?

According to CNBC, 57% of Americans have around $1,000 or less in their savings account, which is far too little to cope with even a moderate emergency. If you were to lose your job, how long would you expect to live on a grand? Another 12% have less than $5,000 saved, which is also probably not enough.

Thirty-nine percent of respondents have no savings at all.[22] Not a penny. Think about all that we've discussed above – what will they do if they need a car repair or a visit to the dentist? Many would use their credit cards, get a pay day loan, or similar. As you know from the chapter on avoiding debt, this is the trap that keeps the unwary on the treadmill and lacking financial freedom, forever.

A quick glance at other Anglophone countries indicates things are little better elsewhere. A quarter of Brits have no savings at all.[23] In Australia, 21% have no savings and 23% only have enough saved to survive for one month or less.[24]

Step 4: Get Out of Debt

The man who never has enough money to pay his debts has too much of something else.

\- James Lendall Basford

'Get out of debt.' Yes, it's easier said than done. But this is a basic, *essential* step that cannot be avoided. You will not be financially free until your debt situation is under control. But don't worry, I'm going to teach you some MMA moves to get you there faster. You're going to smash those debts like you're playing a one-sided Mortal Kombat game.

This step comes before investing for a very good reason. Your debt is costing you. *A lot.* Your wealth is going backwards. There's little point making investments until your consumer debts are paid off. As mentioned earlier, a mortgage debt may be an exception.

Here's an example to illustrate: say you borrow $20,000 to buy a car, at 6% interest. It takes you five years to pay it back. Do you want to know the total cost of the car, including interest?

$23,199.

And if it takes ten years to pay it back?

$26,645.

You burnt $6,645 dollars. Imagine what else you might have done with the cash. The higher your debts and their interest rates, and the longer it takes you to pay them back, the more money you are throwing down the drain.

This is a primary reason why so many people never achieve any level of financial freedom. It is like they are in a hamster wheel, constantly struggling just to meet the minimum payments on their debts, and never managing to actually save and invest money. If you have debts, you must take serious action.

To figure out how much a loan is really costing you, punch your original loan amount (the 'principal'), the interest rate and the number of years you'll take to pay it off into this online calculator and see the unbearable truth:

www.bankrate.com/calculators/managing-debt/annual-percentage-rate-calculator.aspx

Now you're starting to see why those friendly bank/credit card/car yard fellows were so eager to lend you the money in the first place, especially if you're the kind of person who often makes only the minimum payment. It's almost free money for them, month after month after month. Remember that hypothetical $6,645 extra you paid for your car? It didn't disappear - it went to the lender. Your poor financial habits are making someone else rich. There you were thinking your creditors were hoping you'd pay it all back quickly – not so! The slower you are, the more they profit (so long as you are meeting your obligations).

If you are only paying back the minimum monthly amount allowed (an amount which credit card companies keep deliberately low), you'll take a ridiculously long time to pay off the total. You'll keep on paying and paying and paying . . . for nothing. And the total amount you end up repaying will keep on rising.

Obviously you don't want to do this. The sooner you repay the debt, the less you'll pay overall, and the faster you can actually start building wealth. Hence, we must deal with debt before we take a step further. If you have any consumer debt, you *must* read this chapter and follow through. I know some of you would like to stick your heads in the sand and ignore it, but that is not an option if financial freedom is your goal.

How bad are our debts?

According to ValuePenguin, the median American household owes $2,300 in credit card debt, while the mean is around $5,700. The reason for the difference is that the latter measure is pulled higher by a relatively small number of individuals who owe huge amounts. Forty-one percent of households carry some form of credit card debt.

Curiously, it is the households with the lowest net worth – $0 or negative – that have the highest credit card debts. These are presumably poor or disorganized people who have borrowed themselves into, or tried to borrow themselves out of, trouble.

The next poorest group, with a net worth of up to $5,000, have the lowest credit card debt, and the amount of debt goes up steadily by each wealth category from there so that the households with the most owing on their credit cards are actually the richest – those with a net worth of over half a million dollars. Those households with higher *incomes* also tend to have higher credit card debts[25] – apparently that high income still doesn't allow them to meet all their wants, so they borrow quite a lot to fill the gap. This helps illustrate that a high income is not your ticket to financial freedom – managing your money is that ticket. Earning more will get you nowhere if you use it to increase your credit card limit and your spending.

The average vehicle loan owing was $8,100.

Overall, the average amount of consumer debt (credit cards, auto loans etc.) has been increasing gradually over time, and while it declined during the Great Recession that began in 2008, at the time of writing consumer debt is at record levels and shows no sign of slowing down.

The mean student debt in the United States is $33,000 and the median is $17,000. The largest group, numbering around 12 million, owe between $10,000 and $25,000 – but spare a thought for the 2.5 million who owe more than an eye-watering $100,000!

This amount has been rising nationally by around $80 billion per year, from $345 billion in 2004 to $1,386 billion by 2017. The number of older people who still owe student debt has also increased over this time, indicating that many borrowers are struggling to pay it back.[26]

Mortgage debt tends to be an investment and therefore of less concern. More about real estate in *Step 8: Invest Wisely*. However, still owing a mortgage in old age when the house really ought to be paid off for retirement *is* a problem. According to Money.com, those aged 55-64 still owe an average of $108,000 in overall debt, and the lion's share of that is housing loans.

This figure encompasses those who owe nothing at all. If you just consider actual borrowers, the results are shocking: those in debt aged 55-64 owe, on average, an astounding *half a million dollars* – and this barely decreases over time.[27] How could it? Older people are less able to earn an income in order to pay off their debts.

Further, CNBS reports that 23% of Americans are using credit to pay for everyday necessities such as rent, food and utility bills.[28] Needing credit for such ongoing expenses is a sure sign that one's finances are not under control.

A quick glance at OECD data indicates that other developed countries, while perhaps not taking on the same level of student debt as the United States, are just as indebted overall. Every major English-speaking country has a *higher* level of debt than the US as a percentage of disposable income, with Australia having the very highest – probably due to insane house prices. And for the record, Denmark's debt level was even higher than that.[29]

Put all this information about debt together and you'll come to a startling conclusion: given the recent increase in student debt, in coming years many of today's younger generation are likely to be even more indebted than today's older people, utterly destroying their chances of achieving any kind of financial freedom, including a comfortable retirement.

Unless, like you, they follow the steps outlined in this book.

There are two ways of dealing with your debt situation.

Method A: sort it out yourself, using the system I will outline in a moment.

Method B: throw your hands in the air, admit that you're totally out of your depth, and get professional help.

If you know exactly what your debts are, what the rates of interest are (or you can find this information easily enough), and are already making some progress towards paying them off, Method A might be right for you.

If you are unsure about exactly how much you owe or at what rate, and you are too afraid to open those angry, registered mail envelopes that regularly appear, or to answer those persistent phone calls, you might want to skip straight over to Method B.

If in doubt, go to Method B.

Okay, with that said, let's get cracking.

Method A

1. Make a list of all your debts, in order from the one with the highest interest rate to the one with the lowest interest rate. For example, your list might look like this:

Debt	Current Amount	Interest Rate
Credit card	$3,300	14%
Car loan	$5,325	6.1%
Student debt	$11,240	4.29%
Loan from Dad	$3,000	2%
Loan from Gavin	$500	0%
Total	**$23,364**	

Pause here if you need a stiff drink.

2. Write down a similar list of all the money you have in the world. It might look something like this:

Scase Bank savings account	$244
My wallet	$12
Under the mattress	$60
Total	**$316**

Subtract the total debt from the total wealth, like this:

$$316 - 23{,}364 = \textbf{-\$23,048}$$

That number is your net worth. It's how much money you have. For some of you it will be a negative. We'll come back to this.

3. You need to continue making the minimum payments on all these loans. However, to get rid of them one by one like zapping aliens in Space Invaders, you'll need to aggressively make extra payments in order to more quickly get each debt down to $0.

Which one should you start with? Pay off each debt starting from the top of this list. Focus all your efforts on this one debt. Put every spare cent into it. If you like, skip ahead to *Step 5* in order to get ideas on increasing your income to turbocharge the process.

Remember, debts are negative wealth and cost you more money the longer they last. If it helps, imagine your debts as giant mosquitos sucking away your hard-earned dollars. Paying off more than the minimum is like spraying them with DDT. It might feel like paying back all this money is costing you, but in fact every dollar you repay is a step forward.

Go back to Number 2 and look at your total wealth. You'll see that the more debt you pay off, the higher your total wealth will grow – even if it is just growing to a less alarming negative number. Refer back to that amount and recalculate from time to time in order to restore your motivation and assure yourself that you are making progress. Pretty soon this process will lead to a positive number. Imagine that. You'll get there.

Once the first debt is paid off, congratulate yourself fulsomely! Get yourself an ice cream or something to celebrate. This is proof that the problem is not insurmountable. In fact, now that you've removed yourself from the financial drag of the debt with the highest interest rate, getting through the others will be that much easier. Momentum will build.

Now focus on the next debt down the list, the one that had the second-highest interest rate. Pay it off. Celebrate. Cross it off that dreadful list with relish. Then move to the next debt on the list. And the next one, and so on. As we have seen, those interest rates are like banknotes sprouting wings and flying out of your wallet. The higher the interest rate, the larger the wings and the faster your money flies away.

4. There might be good reasons for modifying the order of payments. For example, if Gavin is a good mate and you know he really needs the money back for his beloved dog's operation, consider

bumping him up the list. If he's a bastard who once stole your girlfriend, leave him down the bottom where he belongs. By the same token, your dad might be willing to wait a while if you explain your overall plan. If you owe any debts to that large, rough looking chap, 'Tony the Bulgarian', who drives this year's BMW despite being officially unemployed, put him right at the top of your list. You already did? Good.

5. Use this online calculator to see how long it will take you to pay off your debts:

www.calcxml.com/calculators/pay-off-loan

For example, I entered the student loan of $11,240 listed above and found that if you paid in monthly $400 installments, you'd take a bit more than two years to pay it off completely.

At this point you might get a fright. What should you do if it would take an absurdly long time to pay off the debts? Say, longer than a normal human lifespan? Now that you've written everything down and done the math, your debts may seem more daunting than ever. Don't panic! There are still some steps you can take.

6. If the situation appears hopeless, consider contacting your creditors and explain your situation. If this is a friend or relative you can probably do it yourself, but if it's a company then you'll probably need a debt counsellor to help you – go to Method B after reading the following. Don't try renegotiation with Tony the Bulgarian.

Tell your creditor why you're having trouble paying off the debt, make it clear that you're trying your best, and ask if there's any possibility of renegotiating the terms. Be very polite. Don't lie – if your story keeps changing they obviously won't trust you. If they do give you a concession, make sure you get this in writing. Such an agreement is called a 'debt settlement'.

Lenders are sometimes willing to extend the repayment period or lower the interest rate if you're frank and open with them because they'd rather get something back than nothing. Also, it costs them money to sell the debt to collectors (because those guys often buy debts for less than half the amount owed), and sending someone over to your house to repossess your reptile collection costs money, too. They'd often prefer to cut a deal.

A debt settlement will have a significantly adverse impact on your credit score so don't pursue this course of action lightly. It is a last resort. A debt settlement is about the same as a delinquent payment, i.e. when you didn't pay someone back the stipulated amount on time. This will make it harder for you to borrow in the future, and anyone who does loan to you will demand a higher interest rate.

7. Be wary of those debt consolidation businesses that kindly offer to roll all your debts into one. This sometimes leaves you with more to pay in the long run. Also, be cautious about more complex strategies such as refinancing or filing for bankruptcy. These moves are suitable for some people but you definitely need professional

advice before going down any of these paths because of the risks and consequences. If you're at that point then go straight to Method B.

8. Keep the lines of communication open between yourself and your creditors. If you disappear from the radar they will be more inclined to sell your debt to someone more persistent or to try to repossess your stuff. Respond to letters, emails and phone calls in good faith. Keep or record all communication (you can ask their permission to record phone calls).

The coming chapter on increasing your income will give you additional tools to step up your rate of payment. Once your debts are paid off, you'll have a firm foundation for building future wealth and achieving a higher level of financial freedom.

Method B

If you know you've gotten yourself into a pickle and doubt your ability to ever get out of it by yourself, approach a legitimate debt counseling service in your area. You can talk to a non-judgmental professional who can help you to organize your debts and make a reasonable plan for paying them off. They might also be able to negotiate with creditors for you, or to advise you on matters such as consolidation, refinancing and bankruptcy.

Here is where to go:

In the United States, visit www.usa.gov/debt.

In the UK: moneyadviceservice.org.uk/en/tools/debt-advice-locator.

In Canada: creditcanada.com/.

In Australia: www.moneysmart.gov.au/managing-your-money/managing-debts/financial-counselling.

In New Zealand: https://www.fincap.org.nz/.

This list is not exhaustive. There may be other good services available in those countries.

If you live somewhere else, go to a search engine and enter "debt counseling [my country]", i.e. "debt counseling Equatorial Guinea". Look for legitimate services that are government-run, not-for-profit, or are registered charities. Some are offered by churches or other community organizations. Avoid those that seem to be profit-driven companies – those will want their pound of flesh, and that flesh will come from your wallet.

Once they've helped you to establish a plan, follow it with gusto. If possible, try to pay off even more than the agreed monthly amount. Every extra dollar you can pay is another dollar in *your* pocket, even if it is just erasing a negative dollar.

Final Thoughts

If you have any significant debts then they are likely to take years, rather than months, to pay off. There's no way around it. It may seem a long way off, but with your debt plan in place you can now make out the faint outline of higher levels of financial freedom on the horizon. As Confucius said, any man, no matter how slow, will eventually reach his destination so long as he is moving in the right direction. That's what you're now doing.

Step 5: Increase Your Income

A successful man is one who can lay a firm foundation with the bricks others have thrown at him.

\- David Brinkley

It is not essential to have a high income in order to reach financial freedom. I promised a 'poor man's guide', and this you shall have. However, if you can find a way to increase your income a bit, you'll achieve financial freedom more quickly, and/or reach a higher level of financial freedom. As we will keep repeating, it is all about what you do with the money once you have it. Plenty of high-income people are floundering in debt and have no control over their finances at all.

If you ask pretty much anyone in the world how much money he needs to be perfectly comfortable (not rich), his answer will be the same: 'A little bit more'. Everybody thinks that an extra 20-30% of income would solve most of his financial problems.

Look at me. I tried living in the Philippines on $1,200 a month and found it a bit tight. And yet, there are Filipinos who live on less than that and consider themselves well-off. Meanwhile in the United States, you can read articles about middle class families 'struggling' to get by on $350,000 a year![30]

As wise men have told us for millennia, the key to happiness is to be satisfied with what you have. There are probably people with lower incomes than you who are content, and there are definitely those with far higher incomes who are struggling to make ends meet because their expenses exceed even that lofty amount. That is why the chapter on budgeting came long before this one.

All that said, any extra income you can make will enable you to reach your financial goals faster. The poorer you are, the bigger difference it can make. Consider this example:

Mark and Richard both start a side gig and earn an extra $5,000 a year. They put 100% of this into savings. Nice, hey?

Mark has a very high income and was already saving $40,000 a year. Now he's saving $45,000 a year – a 12.5% increase.

Richard has a low income and was only saving $4,000 a year. Now he's saving $9,000 a year – a 125% increase!

The more you're struggling to save, the more significant an impact even minor changes can make.

Let's systematically look at your income and see if there's anything you can do to improve it through large changes or small. We'll start with the obvious then move to the more esoteric.

Is there an alternative career that would pay more?

This will be by far the hardest option for most readers, but let's not dismiss it until we've considered it. Is there something else you could do without gaining additional training or qualifications? Are you able to retrain, and what would the costs be? If you are young, you might find it works out to your advantage to go back to school. If you are an old fellow like me there may be no point. It might make sense to look at how to earn more without changing jobs. Which takes us to:

Could you increase your income within your current career?

Are there promotions or overtime available with your current employer? Could you ask for a pay rise? Would you be able to make more money by seeking a job with a different employer?

Here's another thing to consider: are you able to increase your savings by doing the same thing in a different location? Various professions pay more money or attract lower taxes in remote areas or overseas. I'm thinking here of nurses working in Saudi Arabia, miners working in remote areas, teachers working in the outback or arctic, or ski instructors spending a season in Japan. Have a look around and see what the options are. As discussed in the chapter on budgeting, there may also be an advantage in moving to a location with a lower cost of living, especially if you can work remotely.

Can you hustle?

You may be able to earn a second income. Is there some evening or weekend work that you could do? Are you able to make a small, extra income running your own business, say, teaching piano lessons or making novelty letterboxes that look like former presidents' heads, or something like that? Consider starting up a little business in an inexpensive way that won't entail too much risk. Be prepared to try a few different schemes until you find one that works. It's hard to know what might be profitable until you give it a go.

Here are a few work-from-home ideas to get you started. These mostly involve an investment of time rather than money. Later, in *Step 8: Invest Wisely*, we'll look at investments that require more money than time.

Niche websites: If you're on top of the technical side of things, you might make money by either selling a good/service on a niche website or by using it to refer clicks to other sites as part of an affiliate program. There is a little bit of money to be made in advertising, too. You might want to check out the course run by This is Trouble[31] if it sounds like your kind of thing. And no, that is not an affiliate link. I should follow my own advice.

Sell an eBook: Here I'm more of an expert. Let me start by saying, don't bother with this unless you're really keen to write a book anyway, just like there's no point trying to be a zookeeper if you hate animals. It is a huge investment of time to write even a short book, it will probably cost you more than $1,000 to get it copy edited, and much more if you choose to get it hard edited, i.e. to have a professional editor help you shape the book itself rather than just pick up all your bone-headed typos. Add another $200 - $300 for a professional cover design, or more if you also want a dead tree version.

Non-fiction books tend to sell well, especially niche how-to guides. As for fiction, erotica and romance are most popular.

Maybe that book you've always dreamed of writing about how to knit your own woolen underwear, or that fantasy romance about the diamond-in-the-rough werewolf and the wallflower Stegosaurus, is just what the world has been looking for. Perhaps you could give it a go if it would be a labor of love anyway. If you've hated writing ever since you had to do it at school, definitely find something else to do.

A lot of your success will depend on how well you can market the book via an author webpage, online advertising, social media etc., so even after it is published there will still be work to do and perhaps expenses to incur.

Sell stock photos/classroom lesson materials/background music or images/stuff like that: What it says. There is a market for these things online if you have the skills.

Phone work: You can make money from home by telemarketing, service agent work, or, for those with the right aptitude, phone sex lines and that sort of thing. In the US you might look up Brighton Communications, Working Solutions or Arise. For other countries, do a web search and see what comes up.

Transcription: You type up recordings such as meetings and radio broadcasts. Only suitable for those with fast keyboarding skills.

Search evaluator: You test how well search engines are working or assess social media. I'm not sure how much of this work is checking for donkey-related videos you wouldn't want your Gran to see – look into that for yourself. Check out Appen Butler Hill, LeapForce or search for other services in your home country.

Online tutoring: If you can do something, you might be able to teach it online. The most common such skills would be your language, school-level math, or exam preparation. Have a look at Chegg, InstaEdu, Verdant and many others.

Virtual assistant: Some back-office work is now outsourced. If you know how to do basic admin and use common software, this might be for you. Consider Worldwide 101 or Virtual Office Temps.

Uber: If you have a car that meets their specs, you could earn some income on the side. There are also alternative apps out there.

Other: There are various opportunities available online if you have the right skills, including web design, over-the-phone medical advice (you've got to be a registered nurse, obviously), proofreading, translation, website testing, copy writing, and many others. Whatever skills you have, search online to see the possibilities.

The general caveats for online, at-home work are (1) make sure it is not a scam, and (2) be aware that what you gain in the convenience of working from home, you lose in remuneration. Most of these jobs don't pay much, especially those that require less skill.

If you are willing to put on your pants and actually leave the house, further opportunities become available:

Sell stuff

Do you have any stuff that you rarely use, say, a jet ski rotting in the shed or some furniture that's been sitting in storage for years? Go through everything you own and consider whether you really need it or not. If you don't, and it has resale value, sell it. Also consider selling expensive items and downgrading to a cheaper equivalent, especially if you have a valuable car that you really shouldn't have bought in the first place.

For some reason, people consider selling off their things as a sign of economic desperation and disaster. In fact, it is a very powerful way of generating cash quickly. I've heard of families unwilling to sell the BMW that sits unused in the garage most days of the week because of what the neighbors might think, despite their economic distress. SELL IT! Don't let nosy neighbors or other peers get in your way when seeking financial freedom. And remember – a lot of them are suffering hidden money problems of their own.

A wealthy person isn't the one who has the flash clothes, sweet watch and fancy car. It is the one who, whatever his material possessions, spends significantly less than he earns. That's it. I'll come back to the point as many times as I need to.

Medical experiments

No, I'm not kidding. If you live near a major university or other research institution then this might be a possibility. Generally, the deal is they give you a very thorough medical examination, and then select only the fittest and healthiest potential subjects for the test. If you are not fit and healthy, obviously this is not for you.

Often you have to go to a hotel or other controlled environment for the duration so that they can keep you under close medical observation in case anything goes wrong. You might have to take a new medication or something like that, and they watch you to see whether you turn blue and float up towards the ceiling fan like Violet in *Charlie and the Chocolate Factory*, or have a strange, bloody-jawed creature burst from your belly like in *Alien*.

Who's keen?

Common sense is required here: the reason they give you money for this is because it is potentially dangerous. In one case I'm aware of, they got subjects to sit in an ice bath for hours to see what would happen to their body. In another, subjects took a new schizophrenia medication, and those are notorious for their side effects. I guess there's a 50/50 chance they'll give you the placebo if that makes it any more tempting . . .

There are also psychological tests. It might be a reflex test or showing you different colors to see if there's an effect on your blood pressure. Or maybe on your way to see the colors an old crazy lady randomly flashes you, and the researchers are actually testing your blood pressure reaction to that, the color thing being a ruse to make sure the experiment is blind. Who knows.

The researchers are legally required to give you full information about the risks, though they might not be able to tell you some other details if it is a double-blind experiment. I advise against even considering this option if you live in a jurisdiction where enforcement of medical ethics might not be as rigorous as you'd hope. For examples of horrific experiments in the past, I point the curious to MK-Ultra, the Tuskegee Syphilis Experiment, The Milgram Experiment, the Stanford Prison Experiment or the Robbers Cave Experiment. Search and enjoy.

Look for lost money

It is estimated that there is over $50 billion in unclaimed money in the United States alone.[32] It is amazing how many people have money in bank or retirement accounts that they have completely forgotten about. Rack your brains for any old accounts that may still be around, including ones you had when you were a kid. These sites tell you how track down forgotten money:

US: www.usa.gov/unclaimed-money

UK: https://pocketsense.com/unclaimed-money-uk-5264182.html

Canada: www.canadianpersonalfinance.com/finding-unclaimed-money-canada.html

Australia: www.moneysmart.gov.au/tools-and-resources/find-unclaimed-money

New   Zealand: https://treasury.govt.nz/information-and-services/other-services/unclaimed-money

Other: search "find unclaimed money [my country]"

You're going to laugh, but seriously, check behind the sofa and in pockets of jackets you haven't worn for a while. You'll be astonished. My mate cleaned out his room when he was moving out of home and found a birthday card from his eighth birthday. He'd obviously never opened it because inside was $10.00 from his auntie!

He spent it on beer.

Summary

While it is probably not essential to make extra cash in order to achieve financial freedom, it can help to reach your goals faster. You might move to a more lucrative position or location, take on a side gig, sell some unneeded items or find lost money.

A final note

If you succeed in increasing your income, even if only by a little, well done. This will make both the previous and the subsequent steps easier. However, there is a funny little quirk that tends to completely negate this advantage: people's spending tends to rise with their income. The same person who managed to save exactly nothing when he was earning $35,000 a year still manages to save nothing once he starts earning $45,000, though you'd think he'd be saving $10,000 per annum. This happens all the time.

Even more worryingly, the person who overspends on $35,000 a year and gets into debt is likely to continue overspending and be languishing in debt even if his income rises to $100,000. Your income makes no difference whatsoever to your long-term financial freedom if you are spending it all, and it can even make things worse because big earners are better able to borrow money and really get themselves into a pickle. As someone once said, you have to be really rich to get massively into debt.

Remember, the point of increasing income is to increase the surplus cash available for establishing an emergency fund, paying off debts, or for investing. If you start spending more, you are no closer to financial freedom than you were before you took on that Saturday gig as a skydiving instructor. Stick religiously to the budget you made back in *Step 2*, add all extra income to the 'savings' or 'debt' lines, and you'll be well on your way.

Step 6: Protect What You've Got

You don't need miracles in the West. You have insurance.

- Brother Yun

Now you've established an emergency fund for rainy days. For 183 to 365 rainy days, to be specific, or 92 days if you're still paying off non-mortgage debts.

But what if there's a *really* rainy day that no amount of savings could cover? Like a North Korean missile destroying your home, or contracting a nasty Peruvian parasite that eats the flesh off your face?

That's why they invented insurance.

Consider the following suggestions and think, do I need that insurance?

Warning: do not purchase or make any changes to your insurance until you've finished reading *Step 9: Get Advice* and have received a professional recommendation on the matter. This chapter is an introduction to the issue so that you will know the right questions to ask and be better able to assess the veracity of the answers.

Life Insurance

If you have dependents, you probably need this. It will support them in the unlikely event of your untimely demise. Even if you are in blooming good health, you never know when you might get hit by a bus, struck by a meteorite or eaten by an escaped hippopotamus. People do die, you know. Go look at the news if you don't believe me. Thinking it won't happen to you won't stop it from happening to you.

Even if you don't die, it won't be a total waste of money – and the following holds true for all other forms of insurance. As the salesmen like to tell you, what you get is peace of mind – the knowledge that your loved ones would be looked after if you were no longer around.

There are two main types: term life insurance and whole life insurance. Almost all of my readers will find the former much more appropriate, but read more about them at the site linked in this endnote and talk to your advisor.[33]

If you don't have dependents you probably don't need life insurance. However, you might like to look into the following:

Disability Insurance

This is an important one that too few people consider. What would happen if you were in a car accident and were permanently disabled to such an extent that you needed a lot of care and could no longer earn an income? That's what disability insurance is for. Basically, it is insuring the most valuable asset you have: yourself, which is the thing that is out there making you money. Most working people should consider getting this form of insurance.

Be aware that you may already have life or disability insurance through an existing scheme like superannuation or some other retirement system, be it public or private. Check it out.

For that matter, once you've found out what insurance you already have (most likely life or disability), opt out if you decide you don't need it.

Health Insurance

Fairly self-explanatory. Modern medical expenses can be enormous, especially in the United States. You may need some sort of coverage.

Here there are huge differences between jurisdictions and individuals. You'll need to research what coverage you already have, say, through a universal health care scheme or your employer. Then weigh up the costs and benefits of changing or increasing your coverage. This is one where you will definitely benefit from talking to an advisor once you get to *Step 9*.

Unemployment Insurance

It is possible to get insurance in case you become unemployed. Don't get too excited – it doesn't guarantee a windfall if you quit your job tomorrow. They're not that stupid. Rather, if you get injured, made redundant, or something like that, this insurance can cover some of your income for a certain amount of time.

Again, consider your existing entitlements before getting this: are you eligible for government unemployment benefits? Is your employer supposed to give you a redundancy payout? Keep in mind they might not be able to if the company goes belly-up. Could your Emergency Fund discussed back in *Step 3* be a cheaper and better way of coping with this possibility?

Home and Contents Insurance

If you own a house then you should probably insure it, because if it burned down and you were left with nothing that would be a bummer. Double and triple check the fine print of the policy to ensure that it doesn't exclude any common causes of house problems. For example, if you live in a flood-prone area, see whether this is covered. Same with seismically active areas or regions where wildfires are common.

The following anecdote won't help you, but you may find it interesting: I know a guy who was an inspector for an insurance company. When people made claims on their home insurance it was his job, as a professional builder, to drive over there, check out the damage, and determine whether it was covered under the policy. This is an honest bloke so if you got him inspecting your damage, lucky you.

Anyway, he said the company was pretty good about paying for any damage that was legitimately covered under the policy. Some insurance companies are awful and will twist and turn and prevaricate in order to wriggle their slimy way out of giving you anything. He even said that they sometimes paid for things that weren't really supposed to be covered, which he disapproved of.

Of course, I asked him if he'd ever felt really sorry for someone and bent the rules a bit. At first he said no, no, he just follows the rules. Upon being pressed (because I know what he's like), he admitted that there was this one time when an elderly couple down on their luck had serious trouble with their foundations. They'd lived in the house since the old man got back from fighting in Korea. Their policy clearly excluded foundations but he fudged it a bit to make it seem like the problem was mostly something else, thereby covering them. But don't assume this will happen in your case. I'm wasting your time with an idle story.

Car Insurance

If you drive a car you must have third-party insurance in case you smash into someone else. This is the law pretty much everywhere.

As for higher levels of insurance, consider what would happen if you had major mechanical problems or a damaging crash, or if it got stolen. Could you afford to fix it? Would you be able to get to work without a car? How expensive is your car, anyway?

Most people end up calculating it's worth insuring their car. Even if it's a bomb, totaling it can end up scoring you more cash than the car's realistic resale value. But don't go smashing up your old, crap car on purpose. That's stupid, illegal and you might get hurt.

Other

There are a myriad of other types of insurance available. Concert pianists sometimes get their hands insured. People with valuable art get that covered. Models sometimes insure their faces, cyclists their bikes, cat fanciers their veterinary expenses, etc. etc. If you have something very valuable then look into getting it covered.

Non-Insurance Ways of Minimizing Risk

In some industries, membership of a union or professional association basically acts like a form of insurance in that they help to cover you legally if you run into problems. In some countries you can join an ambulance association that will cover your ride if you ever need one. In litigious societies it might be worth keeping a good lawyer on a retainer (and in your phone) for assistance at short notice.

So far as I know, there is not yet a good way of minimizing the risk of losing half your stuff in a divorce. In some countries, prenuptial agreements are easily overridden in court. Marry wisely or not at all.

Did you know: in some jurisdictions, cohabitating with a woman can constitute a common-law or de facto marriage and can guarantee your girlfriend most or all the financial privileges of marriage in the case of a break up?[34] In Australia, living together for around two years is generally enough, perhaps even less. In the Philippines, six months might do it. I recall reading somewhere that one night will suffice in Brazil, but I can't find a source.

If such a law applies where you live, do not cohabitate with a woman unless you'd trust her enough to marry her.

Final Notes

Remember, don't sign anything yet. Make some initial inquiries and figure out what kind of insurance you might need. Unless you are absolutely sure about what you require, wait until you've discussed it with an expert as covered in *Step 9*. That chapter will also explain the pitfalls of talking to an advisor and how to avoid them.

If your house burns down utterly uninsured in the meantime, well, maybe you should have read more quickly.

Step 7: Plan Your Life

The majority of men . . . are accustomed to be carried along
passively as their own natures incline them.

- Cicero

Right, you have a budget and an emergency fund, your debts are under control, you've looked at how you might increase your income, plus you've considered insurance. What now?

You've laid all the foundations you need to actually start *building* wealth. It's time to think about the future. This book is all about financial freedom, but what exactly do you want to be free to do? Do you want to escape the rat race and lie on a beach? Do you want to eventually change to part-time work, or get a more fun job that pays less? Do you plan on undertaking a master's degree in the next five years? Do you just want to live comfortably and retire at 65 with a reasonable quality of life? Now's the time to start making decisions, because your individual financial goals will determine what comes next.

Make a list of your short-term and long-term financial goals. Spend some time on this one. Think it through properly. You may find that you have several goals with various time horizons. Alternatively, you may find that you have one main goal to focus all your attention on.

Only about 30% of Americans have a long-term plan for savings and investment.[35] Figuring out what you're aiming for is the first step to joining this elite.

Once you've decided what you want, it's math time. Don't worry, it's easy math because we have computers. But beware: the numbers may initially disappoint you. Brace yourself, make a cup of tea, and let's continue.

Future Expenses

If you want to save up for something short- or medium-term like school or a deposit on a house, plug your figures into this calculator: www.msn.com/en-us/money/tools/savingscalculator. If your goal is perhaps three years away, put in a 2% interest rate/return. If your goal is further away, 4% might be reasonable. There is more about types of investments and potential rates of return coming soon.

If the computer says your goal is impossible, you'll have to adjust your income, spending, time frame or the goal itself. This is the chapter where our dreams collide with reality.

Retirement

If you're planning on retiring someday, plug your figures into this retirement calculator: www.msn.com/en-us/money/tools/retirementplanner. Get a second opinion with this one: www.calculator.net/retirement-calculator.html. It includes a field for social security income but be careful about assuming that your country's pension will still exist in its current form by the time you get old, as we discussed in the introduction. If you are young, I suggest setting it to $0 in order to see if you could cope without it. For now, plug in a 6% rate of return for investments of over ten years duration.

Again, if your plan doesn't work then something will have to give. Modify the variables. This stage is all about making realistic goals.

Early retirement and life expectancy

While you may be so young that you cannot imagine ever growing old and thinking about retirement, this time *will* come eventually (unless you walk in front of a bus or don't pay Tony back on time).

To you, the ages 55 and 65 might seem about the same – that is, really, really old. But in fact, as ages to retire, they differ quite a lot.

Research by some large pension funds has found that people who work all the way up to age 65 often only live a couple of years after that! On the other hand, those who retire at 55 tend to live on until they are around 80.[36]

Obviously, there are confounding variables and conflicts of interest here. Nevertheless, it does seem that having to work for as long as you can might take a toll of stress upon your body, while retiring or semi-retiring once you're ready to do so might reduce that stress and enable you to better enjoy the afternoon of your life.

Escaping the Rat Race

If you don't want to wait until you're old to retire, you can still use the calculators above. Set the age of retirement earlier and see what the numbers say.

If you want to do the math yourself, it works like this: *In general*, if you can live off **four percent** of your savings then that nest egg should last you a very long time, probably until death. We will get to the important provisos in a moment. First, let's look at an example. Say you want to retire today on $50,000 per annum. Nice, hey? Let's calculate:

$50,000 is four percent of . . . what? We can figure that out by multiplying the amount by 25. So:

$$\$50,000 \text{ x } 25 = \$1,250,000.$$

To see that backwards, 4% x $1,250,000 = $50,000.

That means you would need about $1,250,000 to retire on $50,000 per year. That's rather a lot of money, isn't it?

Don't throw this book against the wall! Especially if you're using an e-reader. That was just an example. If your goal is to become financially independent, you'll need to fiddle around and figure out what's possible. Remember back in *Step 2* we looked at making a frugal budget? Well, here is where your parsimony will really start to pay off.

Let's say you identified and implemented various savings back in *Step 2: Make a Frugal Budget*. Maybe you started cooking at home more instead of going out, downsized, or moved to a cheaper city. Let's say you got your annual expenses all the way down to $20,000, which is more than what plenty of students manage to live on. How are we looking now?

$$\$20,000 \times 25 = \$500,000.$$

Therefore you would need around half a million dollars to retire today on an annual income of $20,000.

Let's take it a step further. What if you moved to a *really* cheap location – say Odessa, Hanoi or Guadalajara – and find that you can live monk-like on $10,000 per year? People do this, you know. But they are not a lot of fun to go drinking with.

$$\$10,000 \times 25 = \$250,000.$$

That means, if you had $250,000, you could theoretically retire today and never work again. But you'd have to be happy to live in one of those places suggested and not do much once you got there.

Now, to those provisos. Experts suggest that the four percent rule works for most people most of the time, but not in all cases.[37] The main thing that can go wrong is when returns on investment are poor or expenses spike just before or after retirement, which has a knock-on effect for future years.

The best way around this is to be flexible. Pencil in a retirement age but be prepared to work a few years longer if things don't go as planned.

Another risk is that you will lack financial discipline after retirement. Either stick to that frugal budget you worked out back in *Step 2* or accept that you'll have to keep working.

A further risk is that you'll live longer than you expected. You might make it to a hundred, you know. Some people do. Factor this into your plan accordingly.

Finally, living off your investments gives you much less flexibility than having a regular income. When you have a job, breaking your budget means you save less until you've topped your emergency fund back up. If you're living on savings, breaking the budget necessarily means cutting deeper into your savings, which are all you have.

Having tried early retirement, I found this stressful. I also got a bit stir-crazy from the lack of obligations to structure my time. Working part-time or at an easier, less lucrative career might be better alternatives for you, too.

Achieving self-funded retirement at any age would put you at Level 4 of financial freedom. If reached when young, it is often called 'Financial independence, retire early' because this gives us the catchy acronym, 'FIRE'. There are plenty of good resources out there for those who are interested in aiming for this goal, of which I will list three to get you started:

https://retireby40.org/

https://route2fi.substack.com/

https://apurplelife.com/

As I stated in the introduction, almost everyone who achieves FIRE either has a high income, no kids, or both. Having said that, even a middle-income person with kids has a good chance of retiring in his 50s if he starts working towards it early. Use the calculators listed earlier to see what's realistic for you.

Future Dollars

Most readers looking at retirement will be thinking of doing so some years down the track. That changes our calculations because we need to be thinking in future dollars rather than present dollars.

Huh?

Because of inflation, future dollars will almost certainly be worth less than today's dollars. This is easy to demonstrate with a couple of examples: In 1985 a stamp in the USA cost 2 cents. Today a stamp will cost you 49 cents. The entire Apollo Moon program cost a *total* of $24 billion dollars through the 1960s and 1970s. These days NASA receives an *annual* budget of about $20 billion yet they can't afford to send their astronauts much further than the corner store. Prices of things usually rise over time, meaning each dollar gradually loses value. You'll need more of them to retire in the future than you would to retire today.

But how much do prices rise? Let's have a look at some rates of inflation across a selection of countries to get a rough idea:

Country	Most recent inflation estimate
Saudi Arabia	-0.9%
Japan	0.5%
Australia	1.5%
United States	2.1%
United Kingdom	2.7%
Argentina	54.7%
Zimbabwe	175.0%
Venezuela	50,100.0%

Source: Wikipedia[38]

The future is unknown, but history suggests that the annual inflation rate for a normal country tends to average around 2-3% a year. It might be less. It might be more. As you can see, in rare cases it can shoot right up, as in the last three (basket) cases on the list. In other circumstances, overall prices can actually fall (called 'deflation'), as in Saudi Arabia. Assuming an annual inflation rate of around 3% is a reasonable, slightly pessimistic estimate so let's go with that.

Say you decide that you want to retire on $20,000 per annum in today's dollars and you calculate, by multiplying that amount by 25, that you'll need around $500,000 to do it. Imagine that you don't have the money yet (easy enough to imagine, I guess) and you plan to save and invest to do it as soon as possible. How much will you need in future dollars? There are two ways to figure it out:

First, you can use this online calculator to estimate what the total required might be in the future:

www.vertex42.com/Calculators/inflation-calculator.html

Set the inflation rate to 3%.

Second, if you want to do it yourself with a calculator, here's what to enter:

For one year: [500,000]   [+]   [3] [%]   [=]   (you should get 515,000)

For two years: [**515,000**]   [+]   [3] [%]   [=]   (you should get 530,450)

And so on. Note that for the second year you were adding 3% to $**515**,000, not to the original $500,000. This is very important. It's called *compounding*, and it means that the rate of increase itself will actually increase over time. More on compounding soon.

Okay, so let's look at what happens to that required $500,000 over time:

If you were to retire in five years, you'd need around $580,000 in future dollars. In ten years, you'd need around $672,000. In twenty years, it would be $903,000.

Don't panic! It may look like the amount you need is receding from you like a rainbow from a pursuing fool. But unlike the fool, you have a trick up your sleeve to get to the pot of gold. Remember how that horrible thing called compounding makes the rate of increase itself increase? Well, you will learn to *love* compounding. Some have even described it as the eighth wonder of the world. In some religions it is prohibited, perhaps because its awesome powers too closely resemble witchcraft.

In the next chapter we'll look at how to use compounding, as one might harness the power of a supernova, in order to turbo-charge your wealth and chase down that rainbow of financial freedom.

Summary

But before we do that, let's recap this chapter: you need to figure out what your financial goals are beyond paying off your debts and avoiding catastrophe. Let's look at a couple of examples:

Sensible Steve, age 25			
Goal	Timeframe	Today's Dollars	Future Dollars
Deposit on a house	5 years	$50,000	$57,964
Retirement, age 55	30 years	$1,000,000	$2,427,262

Chilled Chad, age 25			
Goal	Timeframe	Today's Dollars	Future Dollars
Retirement, age 40	15 years	$600,000	$934,780

Here I am assuming that Sensible Steve is anticipating a conventional life, while Chilled Chad plans to move to a cheaper country in order to enjoy retirement sooner. The future dollars for Steve's retirement are calculated for 30 years ahead. Those for Chad are for 15 years in the future.

Jot down your own financial goals like this, check that they are realistic using the calculators provided, then read the following chapter on investment in order to figure out how to get there.

Step 8: Invest Wisely

The cautious seldom err.

- Confucius

As an adult, you need to understand investing, just as you need to know how to drive a car, eat and exercise properly, wipe your bottom, or be able to independently support yourself through paid employment. No one is exempt.

You are probably already an investor through a retirement scheme like the 401(k) or Roth IRA (US), Superannuation (Australia and New Zealand), Personal Pension (UK) or the RRSP (Canada). Whether you are choosing options within these vehicles or making your own investments outside them, you must comprehend the basics of investing before you proceed.

These days you can get away with not being able to fix a car or make a stone ax. However, new skills are becoming essential. Financial literacy is one of them.

Just getting professional financial advice, as explained in *Step 9*, is not enough. If you don't understand investing, you are at great risk of following bad advice. This is a serious problem in many countries, and reading the next two chapters carefully is the best way to avoid having the wool pulled over your eyes. Expect this message to be repeated.

Far too much has been written about investment and some of it is wrong. There are only a few things the ordinary, non-professional needs to know. The rest is sauce. Once you've finished this chapter, you'll understand far, far more about investing than the average person, and you'll be much better able to avoid rookie mistakes. You'll know all the basics you need in order to comprehend financial advice and to invest with confidence.

If financial literacy were a martial art, then this book will get you to brown-belt level. You won't know as much as a (good) professional, but you'll know enough to beat up the bully and get the girl. That is, to find the best financial advice and reach your goals.

This chapter will explain the different investment categories and the options available within these categories, including some interesting alternatives that you might not have considered, and all their pros and cons. We'll then look at how to diversify between and within these categories in order to manage risk according to your own goals and personality, with several examples. The chapter will go on to explain how to make your investments, but read *Step 9: Get Advice* before doing so.

This is the part where there's a bunch of jargon and things start getting a little complicated. Stay cool and refer to the glossary at the end of the book as required. If you'd like an additional definition to help get your head around a concept, you can also look up any finance term on www.investopedia.com.

Reread this chapter if necessary. If this material is novel for you, it may be a little overwhelming at first. It certainly was for me when I started reading up on investment on scattered websites, blogs and in books. Thankfully you get it all together in the one place, plainly explained, with common fallacies removed.

The good news is, what you're eventually going to *do* with all this information is incredibly easy, as you'll see at the end of the chapter. Once you've decided how to invest, your strategy will probably be quite simple, and it might only take a few clicks of a mouse or filling in some forms to carry out (once you've received individual advice). Most of what follows is simply background information so that you understand what you're doing on a deep level.

Investment Categories

There are different investment categories. Some, like cash and bonds, are better for short-term investment because they are more stable, but they generally have a lower rate of return. These are called 'defensive investments', i.e. they defend your wealth against the vagaries of fortune. Shares and equivalents are better for long-term investment because, while volatile, they offer higher potential (not guaranteed!) returns and you will have time to recover from losses. These are called 'growth investments' because they can increase, and not just preserve, your wealth. You will probably need a mix of both defensive and growth investments.

Defensive Assets 1 - Cash and Equivalents

Cash

Executive summary

Jargon: cash can include the physical notes and coins in your wallet, money in savings accounts, time deposits (also called 'term deposits' in Australia, 'CDs' in the US, 'GICs' in Canada, and probably other names elsewhere), money market accounts (MMA)/high interest accounts, and money market funds. All of these are in the glossary.

Risk: low. You won't lose any money unless the bank closes down, which rarely happens. The government often underwrites deposits anyway. Inflation will eat away your money over time though, as we discussed in 'Future Dollars'. A dollar today does not buy what it did twenty years ago, and will buy even less twenty years hence.

Return: low, especially at the time of writing. Returns range from very close to 0% for a normal savings account up to maybe 3% for a long-term time deposit. At other times interest rates for cash have gone up to 6%, but that usually doesn't last for long.

The details

Cash is a store of value, not a productive asset. That is, it doesn't actually create wealth. If you keep a few dollar bills in your wallet, they will not breed and create more dollar bills.

Cash tends to be the most stable form of investment so long as there is not hyperinflation. Cash is 'liquid' in the sense that you can easily get at it if you need it at short notice, except for time deposits. You were supposed to put your emergency fund into an easily accessible cash account back in *Step 3*. You did that, right?

While quite safe, an ordinary bank account offers a low rate of return. Remember inflation? If it's higher than your interest rate then you are actually *losing* money. For example, if inflation is running at 3% and your bank savings earn only 2% interest, you're losing 1% per year. And many bank accounts don't even offer that much of a return.

A time deposit (also called a CD or term deposit) is a cash investment for a fixed period of time, often six months or a year, that will offer a somewhat higher rate of return *but* you can't easily withdraw your money. This is a very safe investment but is not suitable for your emergency fund because you might need that money at a moment's notice. If you withdraw from a time deposit before the specified time period is up, you generally lose all the interest for that whole period. Only put money here if you are sure you won't need it in the meantime. It is a good place to put savings for short-terms goals, i.e. Christmas expenses or a new refrigerator.

A money market account/high interest bank account can often be drawn upon at short notice, but still doesn't offer very high returns (at the moment). You'd be lucky to find one paying much over 2%

interest. Most people either put their emergency fund here or in a money market fund.

You need some cash but it's no good for the bulk of your long-term savings because the returns are too low and inflation will eat into it over time. Most people keep no more than their emergency fund or around 10% of their total wealth in cash, depending on their individual circumstances.

Bank Runs

Banks make money by taking deposits and lending money out to others at interest. These days they can lend newly-created money, but let's leave that for now.

According to the rules of fractional reserve banking, banks only need to keep a small portion of their funds in ready cash, because usually only a fraction of their customers will want their money at any given time.

If customers suspect that their bank might not be able to pay out this money, either through real or rumored insolvency, then they are likely to rush to ATMs or bank tellers to get their money out before the bank collapses. In such a case the first in line get their money, and if the situation does not come under control the bank will collapse and customers who arrive too late will miss out. This is called a 'bank run'.

A bank run can be brought under control if the panic is quelled, if the government bails them out (or promises to, which might be enough to calm nervous customers), or if another institution buys them out.

Bank runs are rare in developed countries but still occur sometimes in Third World nations.

Putting your money in a bank is probably the safest place for it, but nothing in this world is perfectly safe.

Different Currencies

Currencies can change their value relative to each other. Over the last decade I've seen the Australian dollar go from about USD$1.10 to $0.59. Some people hedge for this by holding their cash in more than one currency, especially if they are worried about the stability of their own currency. For example, lots of Argentinians hold some US dollars. This is reasonable if you live in a country with an unreliable currency or you travel a lot. Larger banks usually offer foreign-currency accounts.

Currency Speculation

There are some shysters who will try to sell you programs where you make short-term, speculative trades on currencies. This is hard to do if you are not a professional, is very risky, and goes against the whole point of cash as a safe, stable hedge against riskier investments. Holding multiple currencies, just in case? Fine, if it suits your circumstances. Short term trading? It's a scam.

Gold and Other Precious Metals

Executive summary

Jargon: Gold and other precious metals such as silver and platinum are sometimes used as an alternative to cash as these can also act as defensive assets. There are different types of gold you can buy, including physical gold that you keep in a bank safe, gold held in your name in bullion that you do not have physical access to, gold exchange-traded products where you invest online in a fund that tracks the gold price, cryptocurrencies that claim to be pegged to the gold price (more about cryptos coming up soon), or you could invest in the shares of a gold-mining company . . . and then there are all those other precious metals, too.

Risk: The whole idea of investing in gold is to minimize risk as much as possible. Historically, gold holds its value pretty well. It tends to stay strong even when the stock market and real estate are tanking, and it often does particularly well when there's a high inflation rate, or a perceived risk of such inflation. People who invest in gold usually hold only a little so that if everything else in their portfolio is going to pieces, at least the gold portion ought to hold up and perhaps even rise in value during troubled economic times.

That does not mean there is no risk to gold at all. If you wear gold jewelry, someone might snatch it. If you keep gold at home it might be burgled. A bank safe ought to be fine, but if you choose to sell it, you will have to physically take it out of the bank and to a dealer. Hopefully you will not get mugged on the way.

As for those other types of gold – bullion held in your name that you can't actually touch, exchange-traded products etc., these are pretty low-risk in that it is hard for anyone to steal it from you. As for the veracity of the product – where the gold is stored, whether storage can be outsourced to third parties, if such contracts require insurance, are factors you'd have to check for yourself.

There are some gold bugs who fear an end-of-times collapse where any gold you do not physically possess will be confiscated or go up in a puff of digital smoke once the power goes off. Such people tend to buy gold sheets that can be torn off in little squares for post-apocalyptic trading in a Mad Max world, and they also invest in ammunition, tins of tuna, and bunkers on remote farms that have their own water source. Maybe they'll turn out to be right, but this book is not really for investors who are that pessimistic about the future.

Return: Generally, the returns on gold are very low. It is intended to hold its value, not to grow. In times of high inflation or other trouble the price may soar, but in normal economic times it will languish while stocks rise so far that they disappear into the sky. You should think of gold as a store of value, like cash – not as an investment that is likely to earn you a return. For this reason, nobody except those doomsday preppers holds a high percentage of their wealth in gold.

Other precious metals like silver and platinum are similar but as these have more extensive industrial uses, their value might fall in an economic downturn as industrial demand for them is reduced.

Some people hold only gold for this reason, while some hold a basket of metals to distribute the risk. Many investors hold no precious metals at all.

The details

Nothing makes you think 'wealth' like gold does. Shiny, heavy *gold*. We can understand why dragons want to guard piles of it in their lairs, despite never buying anything with it. Outside of fantasy tales and cartoons, no one really keeps the bulk of their wealth in gold or other precious metals. Let's look at why Smaug might have been misguided in his investment decision.

The idea of gold is that it ought to hold its value because there is a finite amount of it on Earth. You can't print or electronically generate more of it like modern money, it does not depend on someone paying you back like a debt, and it does not require a company to turn a profit, like shares. For this reason, some currencies used to be made from gold, or later they were backed by gold, i.e. you could get actual gold in return for your US dollars. This was called the 'gold standard' – the policy aimed to limit a government's temptation to print too much currency by demanding reserves of actual gold to back every dollar up.

These days there is not a single, major currency backed by gold. For this reason, holding gold is primarily a hedge against money printing or other currency devaluations by irresponsible governments that might lead to hyperinflation, as we saw in Weimar

Germany where people had to take wheelbarrow-loads of cash down the street to buy bread.

There are plenty of websites pushing gold as the best investment because of the risks of all the others. These websites, by a wild coincidence, will also have some sort of gold-backed product to sell you. While it is possible there might be massive inflation and the gold bugs will be proven right, it is more likely that in the long run everything will be fine and that gold will fall behind productive investments, i.e. those that generate, rather than just hold, value. That is why gold is here under Cash and Equivalents – it is not an investment as such, it is defensive. Like cash, it is not productive in the way that a business you might own shares in is productive. Two gold bars sitting in a vault, like banknotes, will not breed and create more gold bars. They will sit there and hopefully be worth about the same when you decide to sell them, regardless of whatever else has been going on.

There are those who invest in physical gold outside the banking system because they fear governments might seize some of their cash or other wealth held in bank accounts, as happened in Cyprus,[39] or they might freeze bank accounts during some crisis or strictly limit the amount that can be withdrawn per day, as has happened in Argentina.[40] How likely this is depends on how reliable banking and governance is in your country . . . and *that*, we could argue about all day.

If you're really worried about it, fine, get some gold. Make sure you put it in a safe and don't go blabbing to everyone that you've got it. For the average investor starting out, you probably don't need any.

Cryptocurrencies

Executive summary

<u>Jargon:</u>

"A cryptocurrency is a digital or virtual currency that is secured by cryptography, which makes it nearly impossible to counterfeit or double-spend. Many cryptocurrencies are decentralized networks based on blockchain technology—a distributed ledger enforced by a disparate network of computers. A defining feature of cryptocurrencies is that they are generally not issued by any central authority, rendering them theoretically immune to government interference or manipulation."[41]

I couldn't be any clearer than Investopedia. Remember to refer to that site whenever you get confused. See how good it is?

There are many different cryptocurrencies on the market, and many more will arrive in the future. The biggest, of course, is bitcoin. The second largest is Ethereum. Each is based on a different algorithm and works in a different way.

Risk: At the moment the risk of most cryptocurrencies is very high – any of them could crash to a value of zero. In the future the risk might be lower, as we will discuss.

Return: At the moment there are potentially high, unpredictable returns, but this is also likely to change as the concept matures.

The details

Cryptos are not just for drug dealers, terrorists and geeks. Normal people can use them for safe, online transactions.

Like cash and precious metals, cryptocurrencies are a store of value rather than a productive asset. Mining cryptos is productive, but holding them is not.

Hang on, my reader might ask. Why are cryptos under Cash and Equivalents, supposedly the safest, most defensive asset? There was that time in 2017 when they soared in value – at one point, bitcoin rose 1,900%, and some other cryptos went even higher! And didn't those cryptos then crash way back down, afterwards? Why am I categorizing cryptocurrencies as a cash equivalent rather than as a risky growth asset?

These are fair points. At the moment, most crypos are bouncing around all over the place and don't look very defensive at all. The reason for this is that they are new – people are speculating on them, which is causing bubbles, and some individuals hold huge percentages of the total cryptos in existence, meaning that if they sell, there can easily be a flash crash.

The problem is that cryptocurrencies are not yet being used primarily as intended; that is, as an easy way of buying and selling things.

Imagine a primitive society where everyone trades by barter: I'll give you a dozen apples for that ax, and so on. One day the government has the bright idea of using money to get around the problem of people's apples rotting before they can be traded, or the tricky problem of trading big things like houses that cannot be divided up into small change.

However, the people start to think that this new thing, 'money', might rise dramatically in value as it becomes more popular, so they start speculating on it instead of using it to make transactions. One dollar goes from being worth an apple, to a hundred apples, to half an apple seed, in the same year.

If people actually used the money to buy and sell things, the value would stabilize and it would turn into cash as we know it today.

That's what's happening with cryptocurrencies. In the future, as people start using them as a way of doing business and the value starts to settle down, cryptos are likely to be a fantastic complement to conventional cash and gold as a defensive asset for preserving wealth and staying liquid. They cannot be printed by undisciplined governments, meaning they should not suffer from inflation like conventional money. It is easier to store than gold, and not nearly as heavy.

I don't presently hold any crypto because I have no plans on using it for transactions in the foreseeable future, but as soon as I do have some use for it, I'll buy it.

Crypos are a brilliant idea that I hope will eventually bring down the cost, and increase the safety and convenience, of online transfers and transactions.

For now, cryptocurrencies are the Wild West of investing, but over the next decade we are likely to see conservative investors holding some as part of their overall cash and equivalents part of their portfolio for convenience and as a hedge against inflation and currency fluctuations.

It is also possible that private companies or governments might issue their own cryptocurrencies, but it is too soon to discuss this at the time of writing.

Cryptocurrencies and the Law

Note: legislation and policy in this area change very quickly because governments are only just catching up with the new crypto craze. The information provided here was correct at time of writing but always double-check for yourself, especially regarding taxation.

'Legal tender' means the currency approved for use in a particular jurisdiction. For example, you can't go into a 7-11 in Japan and try to buy distasteful manga with Chilean pesos or with rare postage stamps. You have to use yen. This is why some countries specify that cryptocurrencies are not legal tender – you can't use them for ordinary transactions within the country . . . yet.

Australia – legal. At time of writing, the government is implementing regulations to make the use of cryptocurrencies more secure and to prevent money laundering and the financing of terrorism. Make sure you pay GST and capital gains tax as you would with conventional money.

Canada – legal, but not considered legal tender. GST applies to transactions made in cryptocurrencies. Profits made by actively trading cryptos is considered income while those from long-term investments are classed as capital gains. British Columbia registered the first ever crypto-only investment fund. Further regulations are planned that will keep cryptos in line with other Money Services Businesses.

New Zealand – legal. This is the first country in the world where you can pay salaries in cryptocurrencies! Various rules apply. Cryptos are considered securities. New Zealand's IRS is currently leaning on tech giants to help them catch crypto users who've dodged tax, so make sure you're paying what you're supposed to.

United Kingdom – there are no specific laws about cryptocurrencies, but they cannot be used as legal tender. Gains and losses are subject to capital gains tax. New guidelines and regulations are planned soon.

United States – legal. Regulations vary by state. Not considered legal tender. The IRS considers cryptocurrencies to be property and taxes them as such. Cryptocurrency exchanges seem to be a gray area, with different agencies variously considering them to be commodities or securities. New regulations seem to be coming soon.

Defensive Assets 2 - Bonds

Executive summary

Jargon: bonds can also be called 'fixed income'. Investment-grade bonds are the normal ones. Junk or high-yield bonds are the risky ones you should avoid.

Risk: low to medium for normal, investment-grade bonds. It is possible for the value to decline, but it does not usually do so by very much compared to shares.

Return: low to medium, generally averaging around 3-5% in the long run.

The details

You'd think with a name like 'bond', evoking 007, these would be the coolest, riskiest and sexiest investment category. I'm afraid not. Bonds are a fairly safe asset and offer moderate returns. If I were given the duty of renaming them, I'd call them 'nigels.'

Bonds are basically loans to companies or governments, but they can then be sold on to third parties. That's what makes them a type of security.

For example, Widget Inc. needs some capital to invest in a brand-spanking new widget factory in Vietnam. They sell 5-year bonds with an agreed interest rate of 3%. By buying them, you are effectively lending Widget Inc. money. Ebenezer buys $100 worth of these bonds, so he receives $3 in interest every year. Don't spend it all at once! At the end of the five-year period, Ebenezer gets his original $100 back. Done.

Ah, but bonds are a 'security', which means they can be sold to third parties. Let's change the example: Ebenezer starts to worry that Widget Inc. is in trouble and might collapse, meaning he won't get his money back. Or he needs some cash to buy a giant Christmas turkey. Ebenezer sells his bonds to Warren before the five years is up, for a price they agree on. Now the 3% interest will be going to Warren and at the end of the five years he will be getting the $100 dollars back if all goes well.

There are many complications here that I've decided to leave out for now. The curious can look up 'bonds' in the glossary for more detail. The main thing to remember is that bonds tend to offer a higher return than cash but less than shares, which are coming up next. Bonds are normally stable and are suitable if your time horizon is over two years or so. That is, they are not suitable if you're going to use the money earlier than that. Bonds can do well even when the stock market crashes, which is why it is a defensive asset.

The return offered by bonds is high enough to make it part of many people's long-term investments, but not enough to form the bulk of it. Bonds usually act as a counterweight to growth assets like shares – they steady the ship when other investments are doing badly. After discussing types of growth investments, we'll come back to bonds and consider (a) how much of your portfolio they should constitute, and (b) how to invest in them.

A word of warning: there are some bonds called 'junk bonds' which are generally issued by teetering companies or governments likely to default, i.e. not pay the interest on their debts on time, or pay back the principal when the bond comes due. Junk bonds are NOT defensive assets and, for the sort of person reading this book, should be avoided altogether. When we get to diversification I'll show you how to purchase the decent ones, which we call 'investment grade' bonds.

If someone ever calls you on the phone and offers fantastic bonds that are about to go through the roof, these will be junk bonds and your answer will be no thank you. They might also be selling penny stocks, which are very cheap shares belonging to companies that are probably about to go bankrupt. There's no meaningful difference: take Nancy Reagan's advice and Just Say No. Also, I highly recommend watching *The Wolf of Wall Street*. It's a great movie about exactly these matters.

Summary

Defensive assets help to preserve wealth but don't build it. Returns on cash and equivalents are generally low. Returns on bonds tend to be moderate. Investors usually hold only their everyday spending money and emergency fund in cash, with the rest of their defensive assets being held in the form of bonds. Other defensive assets include precious metals and cryptocurrencies.

Next we'll look at growth assets. Later, in the section on diversification, we'll examine what mix of defensive vs growth assets might be right for you.

Finance Scams

Here are a few things to watch out for in addition to junk bond scams, especially when attending a seminar about investment.

1. Seminars which claim that you need to fill out an application to get into the seminar, making it seem like some exclusive event only for the elect. In fact, this 'application' might be a contract that locks you in to things you never understood. Read it carefully, never put your credit card number on such a form, never sign anything you don't understand, and always sign slowly anything that someone is pressuring you to sign quickly.

2. Watch out for events or schemes endorsed by celebrities. This is a common sign of trouble. What exactly does your favorite Korean soap opera star know about finance, anyway?

3. *There is no urgency.* You don't have to invest in anything in the next 46 seconds. In almost all cases, if it is a good investment, six months from now would also be fine. Take your time, get advice, and don't let anyone pressure you into signing up for, or investing in, anything in a big hurry.

4. Promises of unrealistic returns. As the cliché goes, 'If it seems too good to be true, it probably is.' There is no investment that will offer a risk-free, guaranteed return of 10% or more per year. The highest safe, fixed return you might get is around 5-6% if interest rates are high, and the highest fixed but risky return you might get is around 12%. Higher returns are possible on the stock market but these are extremely variable, not fixed, and they are risky. Anyone promising you more than that is a dirty liar, and you can tell him I said that.

5. Pyramid schemes. This is any scam that requires finding an infinite supply of new members to contribute their money in order to work. In its simplest form, you tell two friends to give you $100. They then each tell three friends to give them $100. You have $200, they have net $200. Then those friends go out and find four more friends to give them money, telling them this is a guaranteed way of everyone making $200 for nothing.

In reality, pyramid schemes are much more complex, but any system that simply takes money from Peter to pay Paul is not an investment, and will never work in the long run because you'll eventually run out of new fools.

Some programs that involve selling items to your peer group, called 'multi-level marketing', might also qualify as pyramid schemes. I will not name names because those guys are litigious, but my worthy reader is advised to investigate these for himself.

6. Ponzi schemes. These are very similar to pyramid schemes, but they take the form of a mountebank pretending to invest your money for you but instead spending it on the high life, and paying you a return only from the money coming in from new investors. He always gets exposed once he can no longer entice any new money to come in or when too many people want to get their money out at the same time. The most infamous Ponzi scheme in recent times was one run by Bernie Madoff.[42]

6. Crooks and fakes. Check up on the presenter or shill – has he or she ever been convicted of a criminal offense or been barred from being on the board of a company or from selling certain financial products? A quick web search will help you to check.

Are your presenter's qualifications and/or certifications legitimate? Again, the internet makes this quick and easy to verify.

Unfortunately, we are only scratching the surface of the scams out there. This section was inspired by an article on Tom Antion's public speaking site.[43]

There will be more about seminar scams in the section on real estate.

Growth Assets

Overview

Growth assets, as the name suggests, are the ones that will actually grow your wealth over time according to the magic of compounding returns, which we'll explain in detail soon.

This is the sharp end of investing. In order to reach Financial Freedom Levels 3 (could work part time) or 4 (could cease working altogether), even if just for retirement in old age without depending on a precarious government pension, you will need to hold plenty of growth assets over a long period of time.

This chapter will explain how shares work, and how best to invest in them. We will also examine alternative growth assets such as real estate, peer-to-peer lending, laundromats, and royalties.

Your Risk Profile

Throughout this section you will need to consider your 'risk profile' – low, medium or high. Growth assets tend to be volatile and it is possible to lose a lot of money, though you ought to enjoy strong gains so long as you don't panic and stay with them for the long term, as we are about to discuss.

How comfortable are you with this? Here is a guide for a 30-year-old who has plenty of time to ride out fluctuations in the market:

Risk Profile	Description
Ultra-low	Hide cash under the bed and guard it 24/7 with a bazooka.
Low	60:40 split of growth to defensive assets.
Medium	80:20 split of growth to defensive assets.
High	100% growth assets (aside from your emergency fund).
Ultra-high	Put it all on red!

Note that even those with a low risk profile will need considerable growth assets, otherwise they will run into the much greater risk of not keeping up with inflation and being unable to comfortably retire. Once one is nearing retirement this table changes, but that is not our concern here.

Keep this risk profile in mind when we discuss the benefits and pitfalls of shares.

What is Most Important?

Some people get carried away with figuring out how to squeeze a few extra percentage points of return out of their growth investments. But think about it: if you invest $100,000 and get a year-end return of 9% instead of 6% through your genius and painstaking research, that's only $3,000 extra. You could *easily* have earned that much with the methods suggested back in the chapter about increasing your income.

Early in life I made a moderate financial mistake which cost me about $2,000 in lower returns. I reproved myself for being so wasteful.

On the other hand, I noticed that despite my mistake I still had a lot more money than most of my friends. How could this be?

The reason I was still ahead of my friends is because they were saving and investing less, and drinking a lot more. This illustrates how important it is to get the basics right, and how much less important it is to invest perfectly.

As stated earlier, it might not be necessary to increase your income in order to reach financial freedom. However, if you can do so, and if you invest the surplus, it will make far more of a difference than spending the equivalent amount of time and effort paining over the very best investments to make. Don't believe what the get-rich-quick shills tell you: getting a job is a very good way to make money.

To drive the point home: a millionaire living off his investments at 4% will enjoy an annual income of $40,000. That is slightly less than the median US male full-time earnings. Not so amazing, huh?

Consistently and diligently saving and investing your surplus income over a long time frame makes far more of a difference to your overall wealth than the precise rate of return that you achieve.[44] That's why the steps on budgeting and income came first.

It is not *just* investing that helps you to get ahead – it is a mix of all the strategies outlined in this book. For this reason, don't fall into the trap of ignoring income, budgeting etc. and only try to outperform everyone else on stock market returns or on any alternative growth asset. Continue to follow all the previous steps towards financial freedom, choose the investment approach that works best for you, diversify, stick to the plan, and let time and self-control easily do what even a clever person's brainpower and effort can struggle to achieve: grow your wealth gradually in the long run.

Advertisements for Investments

You will see advertisements for various forms of growth assets all over the place – new real estate developments, big-name managed funds, schemes endorsed by celebrities, web advertisements for gold because it's about to go through the roof, stock-market floats of cool companies that you know from using their services, and many others.

Ignore it all.

Read this chapter carefully, get independent advice, and then stick to your own plan. I cannot think of a single thing you could hope to gain by taking any notice of advertisements or hype for particular investments. Go looking for your own investments once you know what you're doing – don't just put your money into the investments that come looking for you.

I would not quite go so far as to say that investment products that need to advertise are necessarily lower quality – I guess some of them are fine, though I cannot recall seeing any particularly good ones advertised lately. What I can more safely say is that there's no reason they would be better than the investment options you'll read about in this chapter, even though they are not promoted by any handsome athletes.

Avoid flashy gimmicks and stick steadfastly to your own long-term strategy.

Growth Assets 1: Shares

Executive summary

Jargon: Shares can also be called 'stocks' or 'equities'. Together with bonds, they can be called 'securities' because they can be sold on to third parties. Purchasing shares means to own a part-share of a company, as opposed to lending a company money, as with bonds. If you bought 100% of all Toyota shares, you would *own* Toyota. I expect that my readers will only own tiny little slivers of many different companies.

Risk: high. You could lose money, especially in the short term. For the record, let's look at the historical worst-case scenario (which might yet be beaten): if you invested $1,000 at the worst moment possible, in April 1929, your investment would have plunged to about $352 by October, 1932. Including reinvested dividends, it would have taken more than 7 years to get your full $1,000 back.[45]

The worst day ever was the 'Black Monday' event of 1987 in which the stock market lost 22% of its value in one day! On the other hand, the stock market rose by about 33% over 1995. Shares are the roller coaster of investments.

Return: potentially high. To nominate an average return is a tricky issue because it's easy to manipulate the data depending on which index you use, together with the start and end dates. The average returns for the years 1932-2006 are going to be way better than those for 1929-2009, because the first set of data would conveniently skip the big falls of the Great Depression that began in 1929, and the Great Recession that began in 2007.

According to Investopedia, the S&P 500 averaged about 8% per annum from 1957-2018.[46] I reckon this figure is as good as any: the S&P 500 is the biggest index, 1957 was the year it began following 500 stocks, it is fairly modern, and the period contains some representative downturns.

Some might argue that it is biased as it skips the 2020 crash that is occurring as we go to print, but such events are too recent to have been properly incorporated.

I also like that this is one of the lower calculations of average stock market returns. One should always keep expectations conservative. In fact, for the purposes of this book, let's assume stock market returns of just six or seven percent over the long run.

Keep in mind that stock market returns are wildly volatile, even over rolling 20-year periods. In addition, past performance is no guarantee of future performance. Just because we got 8% returns over the last 60-odd years does not mean that we'll get the same outcome over the next 60 years. We might get 12%, instead. Or 5%. Who knows.

You must understand that the value of your shares may plummet at any moment, in a way that cash and bonds will not. Shares carry with them a high level of risk.

There is a simple way of managing this risk: *time*. If you invest in shares for only one year, there is a very high chance that a stock market downturn will mean that you suffer a loss. Over five years, it is still pretty risky. Once you get up to ten years you will probably be okay because that ought to be enough time to recover from any downturns. However, keep in mind that the worst ever ten-year period was 1928-1938, when the stock market lost an average of 1.3% per year. That's what a Great Depression will do to you. But cheer up – the best ever ten-year period was 1918-1928, when the market rose an average of almost 20% per year.

How long is long enough? The best, and most annoying, answer is: the longer the better. Ten years is the bare minimum. Fifteen years is good, but not as good as twenty years. If you lived long enough, two hundred years would be fantastic. If they ever invent life-extension technologies, we're all going to be rich.

You should be investing in shares for as long as possible in order to deal with the inevitable downturns. If you are in your twenties and investing for your retirement, shares could be a good place to put your money. If you are saving up for this year's Christmas presents, put your money somewhere else.

The details

Shares, not bonds, are the exciting, high-octane asset class. They are the movie hero dodging bullets and jumping from planes. Shares often get into terrible scrapes, like getting tied down with a laser moving towards them, but they usually triumph in the end. Or at least survive. To see why, we must first learn what they are.

There are two types of company: a private company and a public company. It is the latter that you can invest in on the stock market by buying shares in that company. To understand one, you must understand both.

An example of a well-known private company is PricewaterhouseCoopers. Ordinary people like us can't buy shares in the company on a stock market. It's kind of like an exclusive nightclub. To get into Club PricewaterhouseCoopers, you may need to get your name on the door, that is, to be an institutional or high net worth investor. If you turn up with your $5,000 trying to invest, the burly bouncer will look you up and down, sneer, and say, "Not with those shoes, bro."

This is called 'private equity', and your exclusion is no big problem. When we come back to it later, I'll tell you to give it a miss anyway.

An example of a public company is Apple. It's more like a Starbucks café – anyone can stroll in any time, regardless of who you are or how little you have to invest. Even if you're not wearing a tuxedo and monocle, you can easily purchase shares in Apple. Press a few buttons online and it's done. The vast majority of big companies you already know are publicly listed companies.

If a private company or business goes bankrupt, the owners must use their own resources to pay back creditors. They might lose their house. On the other hand, a public company has 'limited liability', which means that shareholders only lose the money they have invested in it, nothing more. If you invest $10,000 in Acme shares and it goes bust, you only lose your $10,000. You don't also have to sell your house or other possessions in order to pay back any remaining debts the defunct company may owe. This is why such companies can have 'Ltd.' after their names, in some countries. It tells everyone what kind of company it is and what they can expect in the case of a bankruptcy.

Further confusing matters, some countries also allow a form of limited liability private company that is not listed on the stock market.

A publicly listed company – one that has its shares available for trading on the stock market – is subject to additional regulation. The specifics depend on the jurisdiction, but this may mean additional reporting requirements (i.e. of profits, liabilities, number of women or minorities hired etc.) or the company may be restricted in how much its CEO can be paid.

Public companies are usually required to hold annual shareholder meetings where any stockholder can attend and ask questions, though in some countries the rules have been changed to increase the amount of stock you must own to gain entrance as some activist shareholders were buying a very small number of shares just to go along and ask pointed questions about environment standards, union rights and that kind of thing.

Companies often start out private but later 'go public' when they need capital to grow. Being private and having just a few investors is suitable for the start-up phase, but once companies need a lot of money to expand, selling public shares is a common way to do this.

Are you scratching your head? Before we go any further, I remind the reader of something mentioned earlier: actually investing in shares and bonds is incredibly easy. I will show you how soon. Don't worry yourself about that while you're getting confused over the following convoluted details. This is mostly background information so you can understand what's happening under the hood.

Shares are the riskiest and potentially most rewarding mainstream form of investment, alongside real estate. A share is where you buy a part, or 'share', of a company; that is, you actually become a part owner. Though it may be only a tiny little microscopic part.

There are basically two ways you can make money from shares, (a) when the company pays out a dividend to stockholders or (b) if the share price rises.

(a) Dividends

A public company's main purpose is to generate a return for its shareholders. Sometimes they do this by paying out a dividend. This usually means that they have generated good earnings and are sharing the spoils with their investors. Some companies regularly pay out dividends – mostly large, well-established companies whose shares are called 'blue-chip' stocks. Examples include IBM, Coca-Cola and, erm, Boeing. The term comes from high-value casino chips and its first recorded use, would you believe, was during the inauspicious year of 1929.

If a company is struggling, it might reduce dividends or not pay them out at all. Conversely, there are cases where a company will make dividend payments that are higher than its actual profits in order to keep shareholders happy.

(b) Share Price

A company's share price might rise because there has been an increase in earnings per share, and thus an increase in underlying value. The share price might also rise if investors think that its prospects for future growth and returns have improved. For example, imagine that Acme Inc. is a startup with a bold new design for cheaper, more reliable widgets. It floats on the stock exchange, and the share price is modest because no one knows for sure whether this idea will work or not.

Fast forward ten years, AcmeWidge™ technology dominates the market for widgets and all its competitors are struggling to catch up. Now that Acme Inc. is generating strong yearly profits, the share price will be much higher than it was before. Those people who took a risk on it in the early years and bought cheap shares will have been rewarded with a very strong return on their investment. When they sell their shares, they will make a sizeable profit. However, the company might equally have failed if the technology had not worked and its share price may have fallen to zero.

A company might also increase its share price by using its profits to conduct a 'share buy-back' – as the name suggests, it buys back its own shares. If there are fewer shares on the market, then each share remaining is worth more. As with dividends, it is possible for a company to buy back shares to a value greater than its actual profits.

You can only profit from an increase in the share price if you actually sell the shares once they are more valuable than when you bought them. If the share price starts at $0.43 each, then goes up to $4.89, then falls back to $0.22, you only made profit if you sold them when they were high. If you held on to them after they fell back down lower than they started, you end up with a loss. The earlier profit was only a 'paper' profit, not a 'realized' profit – on paper you had the money, but you never really had the money because you didn't sell. Nevertheless, this book will soon explain that holding shares for the long term is a better strategy than trying to quickly sell them as soon as the price jumps.

Not all profits go straight to shareholders in the form of dividends or share buybacks. The company might also invest in new equipment or research and development. Google dedicates about 13% of revenue to such research, much of it top secret. This can help the long-term competitiveness of the business, which in turn can help the share price rise in expectation of strong future growth.

In summary, you can make money from shares if they pay a dividend or if the share price rises, but you can also suffer a loss if the share price falls and you have to sell at that lower price. Some companies fail completely, like Enron, in which case the value of your investment in that company falls to $0.00 and you never see your money again.

A bond is a loan, so the company is supposed to pay you back the agreed amount. If the company goes bankrupt, you are fairly high on the list of creditors so you might get some of your money back. Shareholders, on the other hand, are considered part-owners of the company and are therefore dead last on the list of people to get paid back in the event that it goes belly-up. You aren't owed money – you part-own the entity that *owes* money! This is what makes it the riskiest investment. However, as stated, a publicly listed company has limited liability. You can only lose the money that you invested, no more, even if the bankrupt company still has unpaid creditors after liquidation.

Few are rash enough to put all their money into a single stock. Generally, people invest in a variety of shares. Once you have over a dozen, the chances of them all going broke is pretty low.

A more common cause of losses is when the share market generally declines in value. That is, when the stock price of pretty much every company goes down at the same time. This happens fairly regularly, and the last big fall (at the time of writing) was the Great Recession of 2008.

There are times when pretty much all shares are rising in price, regardless of how well individual companies are doing. This is called a 'bull run', and yes, that's why there's a statue of a bull near the New York Stock Exchange. Imagine a bull charging ahead regardless of everything going on around it – that's what the market sometimes does.

On the other hand, sometimes the market goes down dramatically, or sideways, or all over the place. At these times, poorly managed companies are likely to go bankrupt, and even good ones might be in danger. This is called a 'bear market'. Imagine a bear raging around, clawing everything it passes. That's how it is.

An investor who is 'bullish' is not one who is stubborn or prone to telling tall tales. It is one who thinks everything is going great and now is a perfect time to invest. An investor who is 'bearish' is not one who is unusually large and hirsute. It is an investor who thinks now is a terrible time to invest and that you should move to safer investments.

You should not be bullish or bearish. By the end of this chapter, you will understand why.

Markets tend to go in cycles between bull and bear markets, with the bull runs generally more than making up for the bears in the long run. Some say the cycles average eight years, but it is totally random. If you are thinking of investing during the bull runs and getting out during the bear markets, I've got a whole section entitled 'Timing the Market' which will explain why you should *not* attempt to do that.

In the case of a stock market crash, your actual losses will depend on what you do next. Imagine Aida and Thad both invest $100,000 in the share market, in a broad and identical way. There's a terrible, 30% downturn across the board and the value of their investments declines to $70,000. Oh, no! What are they to do?

Foolish Aida says, "This share market caper is a scam. I'm getting out and putting all my money under the mattress." She sells her shares, gets $70,000 for them, and suffers a loss of $30,000. Poor Aida! Most real-life losses on the share market happen exactly like this – people sell their shares at a loss either through fear or necessity.

It is what eventuated during the Great Depression and it is what will continue occurring even once we're living in bubble houses on Pluto after the Sun expands into a red giant. Human beings tend to make the same old mistakes over and over again.

Clever Thad, on the other hand, doesn't react so hysterically to the same situation. He plans to hold the shares for at least another ten years anyway, and always knew there would be bumps along the way. He leaves all his money in the stock market, ignoring the screeching news on TV and the mass panic of online forums, and instead focuses his attention on fixing up his Datsun 240Z.

The value of the market continues to slide, and now Thad's shares are worth only $60,000. Perhaps Aida was lucky to get out before that happened . . . or was she?

Still Thad does nothing.

After two years, the decline turns around, and after five years his shares are back where they started, at $100,000. Over the next five years there is a new, moderate bull run and the value of his shares reaches $160,000. By this time Thad is nearing retirement so he no longer has enough time to wait out downturn risk, so he starts gradually moving his money from shares over to bonds.

While Aida lost $30,000 in that recession, Thad suffered no loss and ended up making a total return of $60,000 ten years later. To be fair, inflation means that amount won't be worth what it would have been ten years ago, and he'll have to pay some tax, but the point remains: you only suffer a loss on shares that decline in value if you sell them. If you leave them alone, it might not matter.

This is known as a 'paper loss' versus a 'realized' or 'crystalized loss', and it is just like the 'paper profits' vs 'realized profits' mentioned a moment ago. Thad only suffered a paper loss because he never sold the shares at their reduced value. Aida realized the loss because she did sell.

If Aida did not understand how shares work, or needed the money sooner than ten years, or if she just couldn't resist the urge to panic, then she should never have bought those shares in the first place.

This is why there is no one-size-fits-all template for investing. Whether or not you should buy shares, and how many, depends on your individual circumstances. There is no alternative but to understand how shares work and make the best choice for yourself.

Keep in mind the way bull markets play out in real life: the market falls dramatically one day, but nobody knows what will happen next. It might bounce back up, or it might fall again. Imagine watching the market fall and fall . . . fifteen percent down . . . the next month, twenty percent . . . the next two months, it goes up slightly . . . the following month, it falls precipitously again. Over the last century, the market has taken anywhere from two months to three years to reach its bottom during a bear market and start a sustained climb back up. Sometimes it dips again during this climb – you will have no idea whether it is going to crash way back down again or whether this is a blip. It is a complete mystery.

Also in the real world, people don't invest $100,000 on one occasion and then do nothing for years. They work, save, and invest as they go along, often monthly. In such a case, younger people can actually benefit from a market crash – they lose money (on paper) on their existing investment, but so long as they don't panic and keep on investing regularly as usual, they will be picking up additional stocks at bargain-basement prices, which is great for the long-term growth of their wealth.

Are you picturing this situation? Do you have what it takes to stay calm and carry on?

You should only buy shares if you are prepared to hold them for a long time. If you can't psychologically cope with paper losses, or if you will need the money for something in the near term, then avoid shares. Which would be a pity, because they have fantastic growth potential in the long run.

I was visiting an historic fort with a friend, and as we walked along the 400-year-old, coral-brick parapet I mentioned in conversation that I'd lost about $10,000 that week in a stock market downturn. My friend was astonished that I was so nonchalant about it. I explained that it wasn't a real loss. I intended to keep that money in the stock market for many years to come, so it was a hiccup that I could ignore. I was far more interested in the Spanish brickwork.

Some weeks I might 'make' $20,000. Some years I might 'lose' $100,000. It's all on paper for the time being. The trick is not to suddenly sell everything in a blind panic, which is what a lot of people do. Know that downturns happen, expect them, and plan how you're going to react when they occur. The best reaction is to do nothing – or even to buy up some extra shares while they're cheap, if you have the money available.

The stock market is the wild ride of investment categories. It is the riskiest because stocks may suddenly lose value, and it is 'volatile' – the value goes up and down like a roller coaster, making some passengers suffer motion sickness.

To give you an idea, here are the annual returns from the S&P 500 (the index measuring the performance of the 500 biggest companies on the US stock exchange) over recent years:

2018	**- 4.38**	2013	32.39
2017	21.83	2012	16.00
2016	11.96	2011	2.11
2015	1.38	2010	15.06
2014	13.69	2009	26.46

And last but not least . . .

2008	**- 37.00**

You did notice those negative signs in front of some figures, didn't you? I bolded those to make sure you didn't miss them. This is the volatility of which we speak.

If you had invested $10,000 in the S&P 500 (an index of the largest 500 companies publicly traded in the US) in October 2007, your investment by October 2019 would be worth around $23,400. Keep in mind that some of this will have been eaten by inflation. That is not a very good result for such a long investing period.

On the other hand, if you invested the same amount a little later, in the depths of the crash around March 2009, it would be worth around $46,000 by October 2019. Check this endnote for a cool online calculator where you can figure out such examples for yourself.[47] The random swings of the market can make that much of a difference. Remember, most normal and rational people would have been gradually investing both before and after the crash, which would even out these enormous discrepancies quite a lot.

The point here is not that you need to pick the right moment to invest, because unfortunately that is impossible. The above examples are not a dumb guy and a smart guy, they are an unlucky guy and a lucky guy. Holding shares over the long-term is a strategy that will probably work for everyone, smart and dumb, lucky and unlucky.

Sometimes 'volatility' is equated with 'risk', but they don't seem identical to me, nor to some studying the field. The risk of losing 37% in a year is terrifying, but the 'risk' of gaining 26% isn't – yet both are different sides of the same volatility coin. Understand that stocks can swing wildly up and down, and that the true risk is that sudden falls are possible.

Share Markets Around the World

A stock market is where you buy and sell shares. You don't have to physically go there and bustle your way through the sweaty, stressed-out blokes in bright vests yelling and screaming – it's all online now. If you don't know what I mean about those traders wearing vests, ask your grandpa.

There can be several stock markets even within the same country. The best known in the United States is the New York Stock Exchange (NYSE, the world's largest stock exchange). This is the one you've seen on the news where they get a B-list celebrity to ring the bell that symbolically starts trading for the day, and it's got the *Charging Bull* statue nearby.

There's also the NASDAQ, which is the world's number two. Those letters were originally an acronym for the National Association of Security Dealers Automated Quotations. I hope that question comes up for you some day in a pub quiz.

Here are some other stock markets:

Australia: Australian Securities Exchange (ASX)

Canada: Toronto Stock Exchange (TSX)

Japan: Tokyo Stock Exchange (TSE/TYO; this is the world's third largest)

165

New Zealand: New Zealand Exchange (XNZE/NZX)

United Kingdom: London Stock Exchange (XLON/LSE)

Yes, those stock markets have pretty straightforward names. Later on we'll look at indexes, such as the aforementioned S&P 500, that track what happens in various markets.

Shares – Related Matters

Stock Market Float

Sometimes companies new to the stock market will have a 'float' – there will be an initial public offering of shares. This might be when a private company goes public in order to raise money for expansion. It might also happen when a formerly government-owned company is listed on the stock market. Readers might remember when Facebook first went public and floated on the stock market in 2012.

These tend to be risky investments as the value of the as-yet untraded shares is still uncertain. When we get to the part on how to invest in shares, I will not recommend specifically buying newly-floated shares.

Private Equity

As mentioned earlier, there are both private and public companies. So far we have been talking about buying shares in publicly-listed companies.

A company that is not listed on the stock exchange is called a private company, and it is possible to invest in these, too. They usually raise money from a smaller number of investors, mostly investment firms or very rich people, and are not subject to all the regulations that public companies are subject to.

Private equity is probably suitable for more sophisticated investors than my target audience. I've listed it here so that you know what it is, but you should get plenty of experience in plain old shares, plus put together enough money to properly diversify, before you start looking at this option. Most people never need bother themselves with private equity.

Angel Investing

This is when a new business seeks initial, private investments to get started, alongside advice on how to move forward. This is way too sophisticated for my readers and is listed here only for your information in case you hear the term come up.

Day Trading

Some people invest in the stock market for the short-term, rather than long-term, and this is usually called day trading. This is where you speculate about very short-term fluctuations in the market rather than hold stocks for a long time. You'll see ads around for guys who promise that their trading system is awesome and if you follow it, you'll be able to make heaps of money working from home as you learn how to mess around with options, futures, go long and short, and all that sort of thing.

These days, very wealthy firms with expensive supercomputers and math wizzes paid dizzying amounts of money are already using incomprehensibly complex and lightning-fast algorithms to detect any misevaluation or change in the market, and profit from it. Sometimes they even rent office space as close as possible to the stock market in order to enjoy a tiny fraction of a second reaction time advantage compared to their competitors.

How is an average Joe like you going to make a killing in such an environment? Simple: you won't. There's plenty of research that shows 95% of individual day traders end up making a loss,[48] and the longer they have to practice, the worse they get.[49] I guess that must be a statistical weeding out of beginner's luck.

It's a scam. Do not attempt day-trading or anything like it unless you are already a financial genius – and if you were one of those, you would not be reading this book.

Hedge Funds

A hedge fund invests in various esoteric, alternative and very complex areas, using sophisticated trading algorithms and super

168

clever people. The idea is that they can continue to make oversize returns even when the overall market is doing poorly, hence 'hedging' your returns.

When the Great Recession hit in 2008, 7% of hedge funds had closed down by the end of the year – not a great result.[50] Apparently many of them were largely betting on future growth in the stock market, which isn't that esoteric at all, and certainly will not hedge your bets if you're also investing in the plain old stock market itself.

Hedge funds might have their place for sophisticated investors, but for ordinary investors like you and me they are best avoided unless/until we acquire much more experience, expertise and capital. Again, they are listed here so that you know what the term means if it comes up.

Gearing

'Gearing' means that you borrow money to invest in (usually) shares. These are sometimes also called 'leveraged' investments or margin loans. You can invest in a geared managed fund or you can directly borrow to invest. It is also possible to use gearing to invest in real estate, which we'll address in that section.

Remember how we learned back in *Step 1* that we should avoid getting into new debt? Good. Well, is gearing a good debt or a bad debt?

For some people, gearing can increase their returns. For example, say you borrow $10,000 at 6%, buy shares, and get a return on the market of 10%. The $10,000 turns into $11,000. After paying back the principal ($10,000) plus $600 interest, you've still got that extra 4% return - $400 - in your pocket. Free money! Yay!

But what if the market *doesn't* return 10%? What if, in fact, it falls? In the case that your proportion of capital against the loan falls too low, the lender, or broker, will demand that you immediately pay extra money or security in order to bring the investment back up to the broker's required amount. This is called a 'margin call'.

If you are a very rich, highly sophisticated investor, understand that last paragraph perfectly, could write twenty more paragraphs explaining how it works in much more detail, *and* you have cash reserved in case of a margin call, it might be worth your while.

If, on the other hand, you are the expected reader of this book, geared investments are almost certainly not for you. If you get a margin call and can't pay up, the lender will make you sell enough of the shares to bring the value of your investment back to the minimum required. This is really bad news because it will happen when the share price has fallen, so you will be forced to realize a significant loss.

A lot of people made huge losses on geared investments during the Great Recession. For most of us, shares are risky enough without borrowing extra money to invest in the market.

There are those who'll tell you that you'll never get anywhere financially without gearing. 'You need to turbocharge your investments!'

This is not true. Plenty of investors only invest their own money, wisely and diligently, and end up with enough for a high level of financial freedom without taking inordinate risks. Then there are those who take out margin loans to get a bit more growth and finally suffer big losses that force them to retire later or less comfortably than they had expected.

You do NOT have to gear in order to get ahead.

Gearing can turbocharge both your returns *and* your losses. Be aware that advisors who push gearing are advocating a high-risk strategy – is that what you told them you wanted? More about avoiding dodgy advisors in *Step 9*.

If I still have not convinced you to avoid gearing altogether, at least limit yourself to borrowing just a *little bit* to invest in shares. If more than a third of your money in the market is borrowed, that is hugely risky and it could all come crashing down at any moment. For me, borrowing nothing to invest is plenty risky enough.

Note: we also refer to companies that have borrowed heavily as highly 'geared' or 'leveraged'. That is a separate issue.

Isn't the stock market gambling?

It depends.

If you are investing in a broadly diversified share portfolio over the long term, no. Your chances of suffering a loss over a decade are minimal, and there has never been a loss over any rolling 20-year period.[51] The worst-case scenario was a return of about 2%.

In fact, not holding any shares or alternative growth assets is itself a gamble, because your money might not keep up with inflation and you will lose money.

If you are investing for the short term (<10 years), picking only a few stocks, or borrowing to invest, then you are gambling. Like the casino, this is a game most players lose in the long run.

Shares Summary

Buying shares means buying a part of a company. You might make money through dividends or increased share prices, or you might lose money. Shares are a high risk and potentially high return investment that can help you beat inflation and reach higher levels of financial freedom *if* you can hold them for the long run and not panic when there is a stock market crash.

In the section on diversification we will investigate how to go about investing in shares, and the method recommended is super easy. It is so simple that you don't really need to know three-quarters of what you just read. However, it is good to be an educated investor. Always know exactly what you are doing.

Next, however, we'll be looking at alternatives to shares when investing for growth.

What is a sophisticated investor?

Some investments are recommended for, or restricted to, 'sophisticated investors', also called 'accredited investors'. This is because the investment requires a high level of capital or expertise to manage properly. Such products are sometimes called 'wholesale', rather than 'retail', which means that they are mostly marketed to institutions rather than to individuals, and often the minimum investment amount is half a million dollars or more.

But what exactly is a 'sophisticated investor'? The following outline is simplified – follow the endnotes for full details.

Australia: Someone who has net assets of at least $2.5 million, or an income of at least $250,000 for the past two financial years. (All currencies are for the country stated).

Canada: More complicated, but generally assets over $1 million or an income over $200,000 for the past two years. Conditions apply.

New Zealand: A chartered accountant certifies that the individual has assets of over $2 million or an income of at least $200,000 over the last two years.

United Kingdom: Has experience working professionally in certain types of finance fields OR an annual income in the previous year of at least £100,000 OR net assets of at least £250,000, not including primary residence, OR possibly meets some other criteria – you can read through the gobbledygook for yourself at the link.[52]

United States: A net worth of over $1 million excluding the primary residence or an income over $200,000 for two years.[53] The link at that endnote is for all countries other than the UK.

If you suddenly come into a windfall of money but are still not very expert in matters of finance, I recommend you avoid products that are for sophisticated investors even if you are legally allowed to define yourself as such. If an advisor asks you to sign a legal statement that you are a sophisticated investor, but you think (I would say correctly) that you are not, refrain from signing it and find yourself another advisor. There have been sad cases of farmers in Australia who could technically be defined as 'sophisticated' due to the value of their property, only to lose it all through complex investments pushed on them by unscrupulous bankers that they did not understand.[54]

Growth Assets 2: Real Estate

Executive summary:

<u>Jargon</u>: The terms 'real estate' and 'property' can include houses, apartments, office space, retail space, or even farmland.

<u>Risk</u>: Like shares, it is possible for the value of real estate to fall as well as rise. More about this below.

<u>Return</u>: If you go online you can enjoy reading never-ending arguments about which is the better growth investment in the long term, shares or real estate. These threads usually end in vicious personal insults and accusations that the other contributor is merely a shill for the rival investment vehicle, and an idiot. I'll not get into it. Let's leave it at this: over a long investing horizon, returns on real estate in general are comparable to those of the stock market, i.e. pretty high. That's what makes it a growth asset.

The details:

You might either invest in property as a place to live (and thereby save on rent in the long run), for rental income, or for the hope of eventual capital gain (that is, being able to sell the house later for a higher price than you bought it for).

Your Own Home

Whether it is a tacky Hollywood mansion, an igloo, or a hobbit-hole, many people dream of purchasing a home – a piece of the Earth to call their own.

If you are buying a house to live in, that is a lifestyle choice as much as it is an investment. If you are raising a family, buying a suitable home makes a lot of sense regardless of the financial return you might get from it. This is why I don't like to get into whether buying a house is a better investment than the stock market – your kids can't live in shares, nor can you put swings or a veggie patch in them, so there is no comparison unless you are only buying an investment property.

There are some people who claim you *have* to own your own home in order to reach financial freedom.

I disagree.

Such people often say that having to pay the mortgage each month forces you to invest for the long-term. Well, yes, but if you were disciplined enough to invest the same amount of money into other growth assets then you'd still be doing fine. In any case, if your own home is your only investment, that is a problem because you are not diversified enough – you should also hold some other assets.

The you-must-buy-a-house crowd might also say, you'll be renting forever if you don't get into the housing market. Well, maybe you will, and you won't mind because you prefer that flexibility. Or maybe you'll buy a house later on in life, when you might not even need a loan to do so. It depends on your circumstances and what you want. Plenty of people increase their financial freedom by buying a house, and plenty of others achieve the same without buying a house. It is not a 'must'.

Buying a house to live in suits a large proportion of people. You can use it as security for other loans (but be very careful with those, as we discussed in *Step 1: Don't Get Into [More] Debt*), and retirees find it extremely advantageous for their long-term financial security to own their own house because that is rent taken care of. In times of financial stress, selling the house and moving to a smaller, cheaper place can be a powerful way of generating much needed cash, even though it may be painful to do so. People who do not own a home obviously lack this option.

Also, though few consider it, you can generate income by renting out a room to a boarder. People who live near a college or university often find this lucrative, especially if they are hosting foreign students.

Further, you can even save money on groceries by growing your own vegetables in the backyard. The financial and non-financial benefits of owning your own home are countless.

But it isn't all good news. In some ways a house can be a liability as well as an asset – that is, it can actually cost you money. You'll probably have to pay some sort of local rates, land taxes or that sort of thing – and these can be changed at the discretion of the government. In Illinois, US, property taxes are notorious for reaching 2% of the real estate value annually. At the time of writing there is even talk of raising them further. If you don't like a rise in rates, your only alternative is to sell up and move. Check the local rates before you commit.

In addition, it will cost you money to maintain the house. Houses don't look after themselves, and you'll be frequently fixing roofs, plumbing, electricity, broken windows, mold, and anything else that might need work, and you need to consider the time and stress that this might cause. On the other hand, some people love working on their own home.

A further risk is that, like shares, it is possible for property prices to decline, especially in the short term but even occasionally in the long term. This might be caused by a general decline in property prices due to broader economic factors, or to changes in your local area that make it less desirable. Prices in some parts of the United States have still not recovered to their pre-2008 valuations following the housing crash in that year.

Sometimes a fall in property prices means that a homeowner is trapped in that house: the amount of money he'd get out of the property if he sold would be less than what he still owes the bank, leaving him stuck. That is, the property is worth less than the mortgage. This is called 'negative equity', or more dramatically, being 'under water'. In such a case, selling the house to raise quick cash is not an option, and you are forced to stay there and continue paying a mortgage which is far more than the house is really worth – or sell and suffer a loss, and perhaps bankruptcy.

None of this is intended to put you off buying a house. Rather, I wish to show that the phrase 'safe as houses' means 'pretty safe', not 'perfectly safe'. You don't have to buy your own home in order to be financially free – I have not – but it is a wonderful thing to have, and certainly makes raising a family a whole lot easier. Consider the pros and cons, get advice, and make the best decision for your own situation.

Be aware that real estate agents, mortgage brokers and property seminar people are not usually required to give you advice that is in your interests. They make money by making a sale – sometimes a lot of money. See *Step 9* for how to get a real advisor.

Be sure to do your due diligence before buying a property – what is the neighborhood like? Is the building structurally sound? How is the plumbing? Was there ever a mass murder committed within its walls? For an absolute worst-case scenario, listen to this creepy podcast on the bizarre case of the Westfield Watcher.[55] At night. With all the lights off.

Further, there may be other considerations if you are living abroad. Some countries do not allow foreigners to own property, while some only allow you to own an apartment above the ground floor, not the land itself. Some jurisdictions are not renowned for respecting the rule of law and powerful people may use corrupt courts to take the property off you. In some places, other tenants in a condominium may not contribute their fair share to maintenance, either letting an unfair burden fall on you or allowing the property to deteriorate. In other places, buildings are not built to last, and elevators, fixtures, and plaster may be falling apart after only five years. China, cough, China. Again, do your due diligence, wherever you are.

Presumably you will need to take out a loan to buy the house. Look around and make sure you get the best deal you possibly can – some non-bank lenders offer very competitive rates. Try to pay as large a deposit as you can. This means you can get a cheaper mortgage interest rate, and it also gives you added security because there is less risk of negative equity (remember that?). Of course, for most people it would be unreasonable to save up for too long – ideally you'd love to hand over a 100% down payment and not borrow a cent – but by then the kids would be grown up and no longer interested in backyard swings. Do what you can.

Penultimately, do not fall into the trap of buying the biggest, best house that you can based on how much you are able to borrow. There are no two ways about it: the more you borrow, the more you'll have to pay back. That will either mean higher mortgage repayments, or payments over a longer period of time, or both.

Be reasonable. How big does your house really need to be? How many garages do you require? Is the pool essential? The huge backyard? The Ferris wheel? As we discussed back in *Step 2: Make a Frugal Budget*, the only path to financial freedom is to spend less than you earn, and your house is no exception. Just because you can get the loan for a property does not necessarily mean that you can 'afford' it.

Aaron Clarey published an astonishing account[56] of his time working in a bank in a posh area during the housing bubble. All but two of the lakeside mansions were 'owned' by people who could not really afford them, using unsustainable loans that eventually went bad once the Great Recession hit in 2008.

Owning (or striving to pay off) the biggest house possible does not give you financial freedom. Only spending less than you earn gives you financial freedom, and less expensive real estate is part of that equation, whether it be to rent or as your own home. There are no magic exceptions to this grim mathematical law.

Finally, a note on mortgage repayments. If you have a mortgage, you should be paying it off as quickly as you can. As with those other debts we discussed back in *Step 4*, the longer it takes to pay off, the higher it goes and the bad kind of compounding kicks in. If you only pay off the minimum required each month then you will make little progress. Instead, try to make extra repayments that will whittle away the debt more quickly. Even putting in a little more can reduce the time it takes to pay off by years, and the total amount by tens of thousands of dollars.

Be aware that in most jurisdictions, these extra payments count for nothing if you default. That is, say Muggins has been diligently paying his monthly mortgage plus a bit extra for ten years. Come the eleventh year, he loses his job at the call center and cannot pay the bill. He tells the bank, 'But what about all that extra money I paid early? Doesn't that offset it somehow?"

The kindly bank manager replies, "No, sir. Pay the due amount or we shall foreclose on the house." What is Muggins supposed to do? If you were paying attention back in *Step 3* you'll know that he's supposed to have already set up an emergency fund to cope with this sort of problem. He should have enough cash in that account to pay all his expenses, including the mortgage, for six to twelve months – hopefully long enough for Muggins to find himself a new job. Now are you seeing how important that fund is?

Also note that in your list of financial priorities, paying off a housing debt does not necessarily come before making other investments, as do consumer debts. It's a special case, and it may be rational to do more than one thing at a time. It depends on your interest rate and other factors. If you missed the links about making this calculation earlier, here they are again.[57] [58] Your financial advisor can also help you with this once you get up to *Step 9*.

Interesting Facts About Real Estate

- A home makes up 61% of the average American family's total wealth.

- In Scotland, it is traditional to paint your door red once you've paid off the mortgage. If you pay it off quick, I reckon you should paint the whole town.

- In the 1930s there was a gangster called Charles 'Pretty Boy' Floyd who used to destroy mortgage documents when he robbed banks. He was pretty popular with the public; less so with the banks.

- In Japan, it is normal for homes to depreciate in value and they are demolished after an average of 38 years. On the other hand, mortgage interest rates are super low.

- In 2009, foreclosures in the United States outnumbered marriages.

- There are some French castles you can buy for less than some two-bedroom apartments in Australia.

An Investment Property

You might want to buy a property in order to charge others rent to live there rather than live in it yourself. In addition to the rent, which will perhaps increase over time, you'll hopefully profit from capital gain when you eventually sell the property for a higher price. This is called an investment property.

In many countries it offers generous tax concessions. However, you should not be buying an investment property just for the tax advantage – it must be a sound asset to begin with.

Like shares, real estate (aside from your own home) is a high risk, high return investment. While we can argue about which offers the best long-term returns, don't believe anyone who tells you that investment properties are far safer than the stock market. Real estate prices are usually more stable than those of stocks, but you'll presumably have to take out a loan to purchase the property. If anything goes wrong, you might have trouble meeting mortgage repayments. Keep in mind that if you use your house as collateral for the loan, a bad investment can mean that you lose your own home. That is extremely high risk and should be avoided by non-sophisticated investors.

In addition, property is not so liquid as shares. You can't buy or sell a house in an instant – it is a long and costly process. If you have trouble repaying a mortgage and need to sell, especially if housing prices fall at that moment, you might end up suffering a big loss. As you need to keep making mortgage repayments, it's not possible to sit it out and wait for prices to recover as is the case with the share market.

About 50% of those who buy a rental property end up selling after five years, and 90% never buy a second investment property.[59] This is presumably due to underperformance of the asset, either due to troubles with rental income or with unexpected costs.

But what could possibly go wrong that would make it hard to pay the mortgage?

First, you'll need to find renters to put in your house. Hopefully you'll find good ones, not bikers who'll smash the place up, fail to pay the rent, need to be evicted, and leave mismatched body parts buried in the backyard.

The quality of the renters you can attract will depend upon the house itself, and perhaps even more so on the neighborhood it is in. If the area is not desirable for some reason, you might have trouble finding any tenants at all – even bikers.

Additionally, as with your own house, you'll be the one liable for insurance, local rates, property taxes, maintenance and so on. You could either manage this yourself (perfect if you're a handyman) or pass it over to a real estate company and accept that they'll take their cut – perhaps 7-10% of the rent.[60] If you decide to save some money and DIY, accept that tenants can call you at 3am with a plumbing emergency. This is the world of a landlord.

As you can see already, a lot of the difference between shares and investment properties is in personal temperament. You can probably guess where my preference lies, and as you read on, you'll recognize which best suits you.

Other types of property investment

Another way to invest in property is to improve it. Some people move into a house in order to fully renovate it, then sell it for a profit once they're done. Obviously this only suits people with the appropriate skills and inclinations, and you must know how to do it cheaply and efficiently in order to turn a profit, either by yourself or with an efficient contractor.

Others redevelop property. For example, they might buy a large suburban block with one old house on it, knock it down, build four units, and sell or lease them for a profit. Be aware of local planning permits that might slow down or block your plans if this seems inviting to you.

Also realize that the amount of work and knowledge involved in renovation or redevelopment can be intense. It is basically your own small business. Do not attempt it unless you have the time and expertise to pull it off.

Scams

There are many scams and unsuitable schemes related to investment properties that you need to be aware of. Let's look at a few.

One is where shysters tell you about amazing buying opportunities in countries you've never been to. Thailand often comes up – foreigners cannot own the land itself so there are various complications that the shysters might not fully explain. There was a scam in Australia after the 2008 US housing crash, when cashed-up Aussie investors were told it was the perfect time to buy over there – and were promptly sold, sight unseen, fantastic bargain houses . . . in abandoned, burned-out areas of Detroit.

Another is 'flipping', which means buying a house on credit, then selling it a short time later once the market rises. You pay back the money and interest, pocket the difference, and it's free money! Yay! Does this remind you of those geared stock market investments we discussed a short while back? I hope it does.

The problem is the same: the market does not always rise, and if the house price falls you'll be in a pickle. Even if house prices stay flat you'll be stuck with real estate agent fees and taxes. Flipping should be left to people who reckon they're professionals, and even plenty of those finally trip up and wipe out their wealth.

A related scam, often pushed in very popular get-rich-quick seminars, is to borrow a lot of money using your existing property as security in order to buy further properties. You use the rental income to pay interest on multiple loans, and suddenly you're a real estate tycoon.

Aside from the same hazard that the market might not rise as you'd hope even over a period of years, there is also the risk that you might not find a tenant, or a local council ordinance might slow things down, or something else goes wrong to prevent you from paying the interest on the loan, thus collapsing the whole scheme and forcing you to sell your own home.

Convoluted plans that involve a precarious system, money going from here to there, and everything being dependent on *nothing going wrong*, rarely work. Something will always go wrong, and the only people who can consistently make such a plan work have the vast amounts of spare capital to cope with emergencies. In other words, richer and more sophisticated investors than you.

Points to consider

There are few basic principles that will help us when considering purchasing an investment property. They are too frequently ignored in the false belief that real estate always goes up in value, and that there is no risk associated with this form of asset:

1. Consider getting into investment properties as you would starting your own business. Would you start a charcoal chicken shop if you knew nothing about the area it was in, let alone how to cook charcoal chicken? Do your own research and know the local market inside out before you get involved. The description of property investing provided in this chapter is a great start and will provide you with about 0.07% of the information you'll need. Read some books on the topic relevant to your own country, or take a short course from a reputable provider. This book is enough for you to start investing in shares (once you've received advice), but you need to know much before you buy an investment property.

2. Do not buy property in a country you have never visited.

3. Don't be greedy. Whether for your own home or an investment property, expect to hold property for a long time, and anticipate moderate, uncertain gains, as you would for shares. I've seen so many people lose so much money by being greedy, while their more patient and cautious peers have retired comfortably in their 50s despite never earning a very high income. Getting into real estate is not a 'get rich quick' strategy. Like shares, it is a 'build wealth slowly' strategy. Whether you choose shares, property, or a combination of the two, reaching Level 4 of financial freedom will

likely take thirty years or so for a medium-income family man, or twenty-odd years for an eternal bachelor.

4. Aim for at least a 10% annual return. Assume that you'll have to spend 1% of the property's value annually on maintenance. Remember to include tax, insurance etc. as part of your calculation.[61]

5. Start small. For example, consider buying an inexpensive property in a regional area that would require only a modest loan, or no loan at all. Unlike a share market index fund, managing an investment property takes skill. Give yourself some experience before you get in too deep. Some people who have become good at managing real estate say it took them a decade to figure out how to do it well. Some say it took even longer.

6. Consider the neighborhood and how it might change in the future. Crime rates and the quality of local schools are two significant factors. Don't choose the area *you* like – make a hard-nosed decision about which area would be the most commercially attractive. This might be a new, bland, treeless outer suburb that you would shrivel up and die in.

7. Don't choose the house that you'd like to live in – choose the one with good market fundamentals. Sometimes an ugly McMansion is the best option. In other cases, an old, run-down property might be perfect for tenants in the area. Leave your emotions out of it.

8. It can be a mistake to buy a house with a dual purpose, i.e. as a rental property on the beach that you'll eventually retire to. The

house might be suitable for rental income, or suitable for retirement, but not both. Keep your aim clear and focused or one goal might become the enemy of the other.

9. As with stocks, don't try to time the market. Real estate values, like those of shares, ebb and flow over time, with a general upward trend. However, no one knows when the market will change. Many will tell you otherwise, and they are taking you for a ride. Time in the market > timing the market.

10. You'll need to have a good buffer of cash to bide you over in case something goes wrong. For example, the house might need expensive maintenance. At such a time, you will have to meet those costs while also fulfilling your mortgage, insurance and tax obligations. Consider extending your emergency fund over and above the 12-months' worth of living expenses I suggested back in *Step 3*.

11. As with all these investment options, seek independent advice before proceeding. Never make a rushed decision, especially after, much less while, attending some kind of seminar where a slick presenter wearing a Gucci suit rocks up in speeding Corvette ZR1 Coupe and tells you in highly emotional language that working hard, saving and investing for the long term is for bums, and that the smart money is in highly geared property schemes like the one he's selling to you. After all, if that's where the money is, why isn't he doing that instead of presenting seminars? Out of the goodness of his heart?

Financial Seminars

Good financial seminars are ones that have dull titles (Retirement Planning for Beginners) rather than flashy titles (Sack the Boss and Live in Luxury TODAY!!!!). Good ones are attended by professional-looking, middle class people who wear ties, cardigans and that sort of thing, while the more concerning sort of seminars are attended by hapless plebs in tracksuit pants and airbrushed t-shirts like you and I.

Good seminars are kind of boring, like the long paragraphs in this book where I forgot to put in any jokes or funny stories. Bad seminars make you laugh, make you cry, and give you a massive buzz afterwards so that you want to charge out and make those investments NOW NOW NOW rather than go home and get some much-needed sleep before work tomorrow.

Good seminars are run by dowdy, professional looking people who may be a bit gray or balding, and who are no more charming than your dentist, even if you like your dentist. Bad seminars are presented by charismatic, handsome/beautiful, confident and extremely engaging types who make you feel a million bucks when they give you their attention.

Finally, and perhaps most importantly, good seminars promise little. They talk about how you can comfortably retire earlier or get your debts and spending under control, much like the content of this book. Bad seminars promise the Moon – 'Retire TODAY!' 'Wealth-Building Secrets of the SUPER RICH!!' 'YOU CAN BE A MILLIONAIRE – NOW!!!' One exclamation mark or capitalized word means there is a 90% chance it is a scam. Two cases of either and the odds rise to 99%. Three plus and it is

100% a scam. Of course I'm being facetious, but in general this rule will hold true.

More About Real Estate

One disadvantage of investing in property is that a single house – your own or an investment property – can be so expensive that it might end up being your only investment, thus reducing the diversity of your portfolio and exposing you to higher risk. For example, what happens if you put all your money into purchasing 21 Pleasant Crescent, and then a brothel opens up next door at Number 19? Or a bunch of thugs move into Number 23? Or the main employer in the town – a military base or car factory – closes down, depressing all house prices in the area?

For this reason, I strongly advise that if you choose to buy a house, you also invest in some other growth assets, probably shares, in order to better spread your risk.

REITs

There is a way to invest only a small portion of your capital in property instead of buying a whole house. This is through a fund that pools investor money and uses it to invest in many properties. Such a fund is usually called a real estate investment trust (REIT, pronounced 'reet'). Through this vehicle, you can put exactly as much or as little of your wealth into property as you want, with plenty left over for investing in shares and bonds in order to better diversify your holdings. In addition, these REITs can invest in a variety of types of properties, i.e. mortgages, commercial office space, or retail, and they can invest across many locations, thus significantly reducing the risk should any one investment go bad. For some investors, this can be a good way of getting into property without having all the hassle of owning an actual house.

Most REITs are for commercial properties but some REITs are in the form of mortgage-backed securities (MSBs). This is basically a product made by banks selling on the mortgages they have issued. Check the glossary if you'd like more information. These were exactly what triggered the Great Recession: they were marketed as fairly safe investments, but actually they were built on a house of cards, the cards being people who'd been granted home loans despite not having the income and credit rating to merit such lending. These are called 'subprime mortgages', and when too many people could not pay up, the global economy crashed.

So far as I know, these funds have now been reformed. However, I do not know everything about every REIT on the planet. Check it out and always seek independent advice, as we'll discuss in *Step 9.*

While a Round 2 of the subprime crisis seems unlikely, and would not directly affect most REITs anyway, a more serious concern is how well REITs actually diversify your portfolio (remember, there's much deeper discussion of diversification coming up after we introduce all the different types of investments.) If REITs were good for diversifying away from shares they would get completely different returns to them, but research indicates that the correlation between a big Vanguard REIT and the S&P 500 (i.e. shares) is 0.64.[62]

For those who'd like a recap of their schoolboy math, a correlation of 1.00 means the returns are exactly the same, 0.00 means there is no correlation, and a correlation of -1.00 means that the returns are exactly opposite to each other. There's a short refresher on these coefficients at the link in this endnote.[63] If two investments were inversely (negatively) correlated, that would be perfect. It would mean that while one asset struggled, the other would be doing well, thus evening out risk while not sacrificing too much on returns so long as both are growth assets.

Unfortunately, that correlation between shares and REITs of 0.64 is getting kind of close to 1.00, which shows that REITs are actually giving you pretty similar returns to shares, at similar times. They tend to move in tandem with one another. For this reason, I'm not sure that REITs really offer that much diversification.

In addition, I had a look at an Australian Vanguard REIT fund and found that the main companies they invested in were listed on the stock exchange anyway. This means that if you have an ordinary index fund of shares* you will have some exposure to property anyway, and if you separately invest in a REIT you'll be investing in them twice, and paying extra fees for the privilege. I'm not sure why you'd want to do that.

* *'Index funds'* are explained in the coming section on diversification, or check the glossary if you can't wait.

Finally, some people claim that property is a good hedge against inflation because land, unlike money, is limited in supply. This might be another reason for diversifying into a REIT. However, I've since read convincing arguments that REITs hedge against inflation not a lot more than shares do.[64]

If you really like the idea of investing in real estate but don't want to buy a whole house, a REIT may be suitable. Try to find one that doesn't just invest in shares that you already have exposure to.

Real Estate Summary

Consider investing in property if it's to live in (thereby eliminating rent and generating long-term growth), or as a part of your overall investment portfolio. If you want to go all in and become a professional landlord then you'll need to really know what you're doing and treat it as your own business. REITs offer an easier alternative for the investor who wants a smaller amount of exposure to real estate, but are not essential and may not offer much benefit above and beyond a share fund anyway.

It is not essential to invest in real estate. It is an option. If real estate doesn't suit you, you can diversify your investments elsewhere.

Growth Assets 3: Alternatives to Shares and Real Estate

Most people trying to build wealth content themselves with simply investing in shares, or in shares plus their own home. A few purchase an investment property. Such conventional options are fine.

However, there are alternatives. Here I list a few for the more adventurous or unconventional investor. Like enlightenment, there are different paths to financial freedom. If the Roman Catholicism of shares and real estate is not for you, perhaps these Hare Krishna options might be of interest.

Peer to Peer Lending

Executive summary:

The jargon: Peer to peer lending, or P2P, means that you lend money at an agreed rate of interest, for an agreed period of time, to a stranger via an online platform.

Risk: High, especially if lending for higher rates to those with a poor credit rating. A borrower might not return all the money, or not on time. Some countries have special laws for borrowers facing hardship, giving them extra time to meet repayments or reducing the interest rate. Borrowers usually repay because there are consequences if they don't, depending on the jurisdiction, but do not assume that the police will go knock on his door and get all your money back for you if anything goes wrong. It doesn't work like that. Rather, the defaulter will lose his credit rating. You may lose your money. Some platforms have a type of insurance that covers lenders in the case of a loan gone bad, but if many borrowers all default at once then this insurance will be insufficient to cover the total cost.

Return: There are different rates of return depending on how secure the borrower is considered to be, ranging from around 2-10% at the time of writing. Some P2P platforms lend to businesses at higher rates but these seem unsuitable for ordinary investors like you.

The details:

Peer to peer investments are a very new form of growth asset, only about a decade old. Some of the biggest players include Lending Club, Prosper, Zopa, and RateSetter, plus there are many smaller players. These online platforms match borrowers to lenders in order to make the process simpler and to distribute risk. They make their money by taking a cut of the interest rate, through fees, or a bit of both.

Borrowers wanting money for some reason – for a car, a consumer purchase or whatever – will sometimes use this service as they can get a better rate than from a conventional lender.

So far, these investments seem to be working pretty well – most borrowers are repaying the loans with interest as intended, so there is no shortage of potential lenders to keep the process going.

A couple of things to consider: first, at the time of writing we have had a long period of economic growth. What happens to these sorts of investments in an economic downturn when lots of people are losing their jobs or are otherwise tightening their belts? It is too early to say.

Second, the platforms I looked at do not examine the credit scores of potential borrowers in the same depth as other lenders, like banks and credit card companies, which might make these investments a bit riskier than they appear.

So far, P2P looks like a good form of alternative growth asset for those who don't want all their money in shares. However, don't forget that this is a high risk, high return investment. It is for a shorter time period than other growth assets but is no safer. If you choose this path, only put a fraction of your wealth here.

Personally, I am concerned that P2P might perform poorly at the same time that shares are suffering, thus defeating the purpose of diversifying into them in the first place. I'm keeping my money out for now. I'll watch what happens to them during the next recession, then I'll decide if I'd like to get involved. You can make your own decision once you've read the section on asset allocation and have sought independent advice as per *Step 9.*

Investing with Friends and Relatives

Sometimes a friend or relative might be starting up a business and ask you for an investment. What should you do?

Here the dangers are twofold: you might lose the investment *and* lose your relationship with that person if it all goes pear-shaped, as many new businesses do.

A word to the wise: consider investing an amount that is enough to show your moral support for their venture, but not so much that losing it would cause a rift in your relationship. How much that amount is will depend on your own circumstances.

Or tell them plainly 'no' if you're an insensitive old grump like me.

Other Alternative Growth Investments

The number of potential growth investments is infinite, and clever entrepreneurs are inventing new ones every day.

You might put your savings into buying a café, or starting an ostrich farm, or investing in art or Dr. Who memorabilia. You could turn your shed into a workshop and start building high-end timber furniture – or you could rent out your empty shed as storage space. You could upgrade the machinery you use for your gardening business. The possibilities are endless.

This book focuses on managing the money you already have, rather than on how to earn money or run your own business. If that sort of thing appeals to you, read specific resources on the topic and take it from there. If you make a bit of money and want to know what to do with it, then you can come back to this book.

Let's briefly look at a few common, alternative investments and glance at their pros and cons. The difference between these suggestions and those offered in *Step 5: Increase Your Income* is that these mostly require an investment of capital, while those earlier ideas primarily involve an investment of time and labor. These will probably not require a loan as for an investment property – you can save and invest in small chunks over time.

Laundromats/automated car washes and car parks/vending machines/that sort of thing: These can be a good way of receiving a passive income, but 'passive' only means you don't have to be there all the time. You do need to maintain the equipment, monitor security, collect the cash regularly, manage local rates, insurance and so on. According to accounts that I have read, these investments don't pay fantastic returns, can be more work than you might think, and the customers who use them are often idiots who break everything or make a mess. On the other hand, this sort of investment might suit a person who doesn't want all their money floating around in the ether of the share market and who would prefer a tangible, hands-on asset that they can maintain and improve themselves.

Bars: I know a few people who've run bars, usually tiny, hole in the wall places, for some extra cash. While you don't have to be there all the time if you can find good staff, this investment best suits drinkers and night owls who would enjoy hanging out there quite a lot to ensure that everything is running properly.

Royalties: You can go to a place like RoyaltyExchange.com and buy the rights to a song, like how Michael Jackson bought up the rights to those old Beatles tunes. You can also buy the rights to other intellectual property. If someone uses your song then they have to pay you royalties. Sweet, hey? I had a quick look and at the time of writing, the highest bid for a mix album with tracks by Kiiara and others was up to $345,000. A more obscure album was going for $40,000. Confession: I have never tried this and don't know anyone who has. The site gives you a suggestion about what the return might be based on recent earnings, but I don't know how you'd judge if that is reasonable, nor how to protect the asset against pirates. If you think you do, I guess you could give it a go. Good luck!

Summary of Alternative Growth Assets

I certainly encourage any of the above if you know what you're doing and it suits your personality and goals. Your return will depend on how good you are and a fair swag of luck. As discussed back in *Step 2*, be wary of getting into a lot of debt to start up your idea. If it all seems a bit strange and effortful, stick with plain old shares.

Recap of Investment Categories

You probably need a mix of defensive and growth assets.

Cash is the safest investment, and should be used for your emergency fund. It is possible to hold multiple currencies. Alternatives include gold, other precious metals, and cryptocurrencies.

Bonds are also a defensive asset. Investment-grade bonds can generate modest but stable returns, and the risk of losing a lot of money is low.

Shares are the most volatile investment but also enjoy the most growth over a long time frame.

Real estate can make sense if you'd like to buy a house to live in. If you want to purchase investment properties, you really need to know what you're doing as you would if you were running your own business, especially if you are taking out a loan to do so.

Alternative growth assets include peer-to-peer lending, laundromats, royalties and many others.

Henceforth we'll mostly consider cash, bonds and shares, but keep in mind the alternatives to each as discussed in this section.

Past performance is no guarantee of future performance

Here's a common rookie investing error: you see that Acme Corp. goes up 14% in 2018. Then it goes up another 16% in 2019. You think, I must buy Acme shares, and quickly! You buy . . . and then in 2020 the share price falls by 22%. : (

Just because an investment has enjoyed a certain return in the past does not mean that it will continue to earn that return in the future. Except for safe investments like term deposits/CDs, returns will vary from year to year. A recent, rapid rise in house prices does not mean that you ought to be investing more in real estate. A sudden increase in Megadeth memorabilia does not mean that you should rush out to buy garish Megadeth t-shirts. In fact, a recent rise might mean the pendulum is about to swing back the other way and prices will fall.

Instead of chasing yesterday's winners, invest broadly in ways that suit your own financial goals and risk profile. Don't chop and change according to short-term fluctuations. Stick to your own plan over the long term and reap the rewards.

The Magic of Compounding

So far we've explained the main investment categories, and in a moment we'll look at how much you should invest in each category, and how to go about doing so. But before we do that, it is essential for you to understand what Einstein supposedly called 'the eighth wonder of the world': compounding returns.

Do you remember back in *Step 7: Plan Your Life*, when we were calculating how much money you would need in future dollars, and how compounding inflation made the amount required increase faster and faster as time went on, and how you fled screaming and crying to your trailer and wouldn't come out?

Yeah, you remember.

At that time I assured you that compounding would save you more than it would damn you, and I promised to show you why. Well, here you go.

Let's say you invest $100,000 in the stock market and reinvest all returns. That means if you make a modest 6% in one year, you put that extra $6,000 into buying more shares rather than taking it out and spending it all on pimping your Hyundai Excel. What would happen in the long run? Let's say you make an average return of 6%. We'll calculate this as exactly 6% a year for simplicity's sake, but in reality, the returns would fluctuate madly and would sometimes be negative, as you saw in that section about shares.

You can use this online calculator to figure out how the original $100,000 might increase over time:

www.investor.gov/additional-resources/free-financial-planning-tools/compound-interest-calculator

This is a calculator for interest rather than stock market returns, but it's good enough for us to get a ballpark figure. Enter $100,000 as the principal, 6% as the 'interest', and then try entering a number of years as you please. Make sure to try out numbers >10, because as discussed, you're supposed to hold volatile growth assets like shares for the long haul.

To do it yourself with an old-fashioned calculator, it's the same as for when we were figuring out inflation earlier:

First year: 100,000 [+] [6] [%] [=]   (you should get 106,000)

Second year: 106,000 [+] [6] [%] [=]   (you should get 112,360)

Third year: 112,360 [+] [6] [%] [=]   (you should get 119,102 rounded off)

You see? In the second year we're adding 6% of $106,000, not the original $100,000, because we reinvested last year's $6,000 in extra shares. Hence, we don't make another $6,000 – we make $6,360. By the third year we're making $6,742. This is compounding: returns on top of returns mean your money can grow faster and faster over time.

After five years you'd have $133,823. After ten years, $179,085. After twenty years, $320,714. And after thirty years, $574,349.

Not bad, hey? If you can afford to wait around thirty years (and if this is for retirement, maybe you can), then you made almost half a million dollars sitting on your bottom doing absolutely nothing. Of course, some of this would be eaten up by inflation, and there are also capital gains taxes, but you're still way ahead.

If you continually add to your investment over time as most normal, employed people would, then the figures look even better. For example, say you start with $100,000 then add $500 of your savings per month, and assume an average return of 6%. You can use the same online calculator to figure it out - after thirty years you'd have the tidy sum of $1,048,698.

The actual numbers would vary because of the volatility of the market – it would never be exactly 6% per year – but you get the idea of the kind of returns that are possible if you are able to *wait*.

The key factor, as you can see, is *time*. The more of it you have, the richer you can become. If your financial goals chosen earlier seemed impossible, try putting them back a few years and recalculate. It will make a big difference. Compounding means that time is your friend, and all good things come to those who wait. Try not to die of old age in the meantime.

Reversal

In real life, your returns might not be so rosy as compounding average returns suggests due to the downward drag of negative numbers when you lose money. Hit this endnote for a detailed discussion of why this is,[65] or just remember that compounding returns jump up and down in alarming ways not reflected in those calculations above, and that the end result is never certain.

Keep compounding in mind for the next section on choosing how to invest your money. Growth assets only help to build wealth if you can afford to leave your money there long-term and let compounding work its magic. If you might need the money sooner, lower performing defensive assets are more suitable. However, if you change the above calculations so that there is only a 4% rate of return, as might be expected from bonds, you can see for yourself that you'll enjoy far less capital growth – perhaps not enough to reach your desired level of financial freedom.

Diversifying Between Investment Classes

You need a mix of cash, bonds and shares (or their respective equivalents) in order to manage risk and to reap the benefits of each investment class. Deciding how much to put into each is called 'asset allocation'. But how do you decide?

It depends on your personal circumstances and comfort with risk. Cash is the simplest category so let's start there.

How Much Cash/Equivalents?

You need enough in the bank for your normal, day-to-day expenses plus your emergency fund in case the smelly stuff hits the fan.

Time deposits (CDs) can be suitable if you're saving for a purchase in the short term, generally <5 years. If you're saving up for a car in eighteen months then a term deposit may be a safe and convenient place to put your money.

However, remember that your emergency fund should be readily available, so a term deposit is unsuitable. An at-call, high interest bank account is better.

If you are starting out on your investing adventure and don't have your emergency fund set up yet, do that first. Remember the order of operations: (a) set up a 3 month emergency fund, (b) pay back non-mortgage debts if you have any, (c) increase your emergency fund to cover 6-12 months' expenses, and (d) start making growth investments. If you're still on (c), get that sorted first, even though your wealth will be 100% cash for the time being. Other investments can wait.

Once you've set up your emergency fund and savings for any other big expenses you've got coming up, then you can start moving into bonds and shares. At this stage it is likely that, as your wealth grows, you'll end up having 10% or less of your wealth in cash and equivalents – not because you're taking money out of the bank, but because you're putting more and more money into those higher performing assets. You'll need that emergency fund throughout your life, unless you somehow think you have become impervious to emergencies. Has your car become indestructible? Are you wearing the sheath of Excalibur that protects you from hurt? If not, keep that emergency fund right where it is and make sure it remains adequate as time goes on and inflation makes potential emergency expenses increase.

Retirees who are focused on preserving, rather than building, wealth may have more need of cash for greater stability, but they are not my target audience.

How Much in Bonds and Shares Respectively?

Once you have enough saved in cash, the rest should go into bonds and shares/alternative growth assets. For brevity, I will say 'shares' here instead of reminding you each time that some form of real estate or alternative investment might also be suitable.

Bonds and shares will hopefully give you higher returns over the long run. It can be a bit more time consuming to get your money out, but that's okay because this is the money you won't need in a hurry. That's what your cash is for.

The higher your proportion of shares to bonds, the higher the risk and potential return. A higher proportion of bonds to shares means a more stable but probably lower-returning portfolio in the long run.

A rule of thumb sometimes suggested is to subtract your age from 100 in order to figure out roughly what percentage of your wealth should be invested in shares. For example:

Age 20: 100 – 20 = 80, so invest 80% of your money in shares.

Age 40: 100 – 40 = 60, so invest 60% of your money in shares.

Age 60: 100 – 60 = 40, so invest 40% of your money in shares.

The idea is that younger investors can afford more risk as they have time to wait out downturns, while older people will need to rely on their investments for retirement income soon so they should increase their holdings of defensive assets like bonds. According to this model, you'd be gradually shifting from growth to defensive assets throughout your life. Most retirees find they still need some growth assets as they might end up living for a very long time, and need their assets to keep up with inflation.

No one would claim this is an iron-clad rule. There are reasons you might choose differently. For example, if you are young (say, in your 20s), saving for retirement, and comfortable with a high level of risk, you might consider putting 100% of your long-term savings into shares rather than 80%. In this way you would benefit from the expected higher returns that they would generate if given enough time – that is, decades. It is not essential to hedge this with bonds at such a young age because you have a good 40 years or more to make up for any downturn in the markets.

On the other hand, some investors might choose to invest less in shares than suggested by that rule of thumb because they are very risk averse.

Imagine you are 20, invest 100% in shares, and the market drops 30% in a day. That means that the value of your investment drops 30%. Remember we talked about this possibility earlier, with that story about Thad and Aida? If you withdraw your money at that moment then you will realize the loss; that is, you will actually lose 30% of your money. If, on the other hand, you do nothing and wait for the market to recover, the value of your investment will probably rise back to where it was and then higher over the next few years and you will actually lose nothing, except temporarily on paper.

But are you cool with that? Would you have the self-control to avoid panic and hold on to your shares, even when everyone else is running around like a flock of headless chickens and selling everything? Could you calmly watch your savings disappear, confident that they will eventually reappear? Would you even get *excited* at the chaos, and try to buy additional shares at bargain prices if you can?

If you answered 'yes' to the questions above then the 100% shares strategy might be for you. If you answered 'no' then you should look at diversifying into bonds. While generally less lucrative over the long run, returns on bonds sometimes rise even as the stock market is falling, so they can even out the swings of fortune and give you a bit more stability. Mathematically it would make most sense to put all your money into shares if you have decades on your hands, but realistically you are a human being with human feelings. There's no point trying to wring every last cent out of your investments if the level of risk is going to keep you awake at night worrying about it. Sleeping well is important for your health.

But how much should you diversify into bonds? That is a good question, and one that you will need to answer for yourself. If you want to take the edge off a potential market downturn, 10-20% in bonds ought to do the trick. If you really can't afford or stomach a large downturn, consider putting 20-40% into bonds.

As stated, you should move towards holding a greater proportion of your wealth in bonds as you near your target retirement age.

But be careful! There's yet another risk to consider, and that is the possibility that your funds won't make the distance. Remember, many people live a really long time these days. You might last until you're ninety-five. Could you afford to live that long? You need to balance the need for stability against the need for higher-than-inflation returns. Don't wimp out too much by hiding in bonds. If you're in your 30s, 30% is heaps. In your 20s, 20% is a lot. Zero percent would be fine for most young people.

Remember back when we were talking about the 4% rule? To recap, you'll need to be able to live off around 4% of your assets annually in order to reach Level 4 of financial freedom, i.e. retirement. That figure assumes you will have a mix of shares and bonds. If you have it all in bonds and cash then you'll need to take out less than 4% to make it last the distance.

You should ask for further suggestions on how much to put into different investment classes once we get to *Step 9: Seek Advice*.

Some Sample Asset Allocation Strategies

Young Gun

This is for someone who has recently started working, is not risk averse, and who is saving for retirement in the distant future:

Savings Account (for daily expenses):
$3,000

High-interest, At-Call Account (emergency fund):
$20,000

Shares:
$50,000

Note that the Young Gun has already set up his emergency fund before investing in shares. First things first. Also note that he's not currently saving for any near-term expenses, including a deposit on a house. If he were, that would be in cash (<5yrs) or bonds (>5yrs), and he would probably put that together before he began investing in shares. As it is, all future savings achieved in his budget will be added to shares, so that portion will grow over time.

See how simple this strategy this is. While diversity is good, simplicity is also good. We'll talk more about that at the end of the chapter.

This is for someone who is constitutionally ill-suited to share market investment and would rather have more tangible growth assets. Only a small minority of people would fit into this category but, just so you know, it's an option:

Savings Account (for daily expenses):
$3,000

High-interest, At-Call Account (emergency fund):
$20,000

Laundromats:
$30,000

Vending Machines:
$10,000

Peer to Peer Lending:
$10,000

Note that the self-starter is not putting it all on red – his growth assets are spread out among three different categories, even though they are all alternative.

For someone who cannot psychologically cope with the raw volatility of shares, even if young, the following is a more moderate strategy:

Savings Account (for daily expenses):
$3,000

High-interest, At-Call Account (emergency fund):
$30,000

Shares:
$30,000

Bonds:
$10,000

The Worry-Wart has diversified into bonds so that there is less overall volatility in his portfolio, and he has also upped the amount in his emergency fund. This strategy will likely deliver lower returns over the long run, but if you can't handle the heat, stay out of the kitchen. Note that the Worry-Wart still has a significant portion of growth assets – without them, he will never reach his financial goals, and then he'd be worried about that. Also note that as we get older, our timeframe shortens and all of our portfolios start to look as conservative than this one, or more so.

Diversify Within Investment Classes

So far we have looked at diversifying between defensive and growth assets in order to set an appropriate level of risk.

To further spread that risk, it is essential to diversify *within* each category, as well. For example, it would be madness to hold only one share. The company might go bankrupt. It is much safer to invest across many shares.

In this section we'll go through each class of investments and show how to diversify within it in order to manage risk.

Cash and Alternatives

You might not need to diversify much within this asset class as it is already pretty safe. If you don't trust the banking system in your country you may want to have accounts with different banks, or with overseas banks. If you are worried about the value of your home nation's currency you may want to diversify out of that. Those worried about inflation in general may want to have some gold and/or cryptocurrencies for peace of mind.

Here are some samples:

Steady Jeff

Savings Account: (for everyday expenses) $3,000

High-Interest Account (emergency fund) $20,000

Can't get simpler than that. This is fine for most people. Note that you'll need at least one account for normal shopping, bills etc. that is easy to access, and which you'll top up from your income each month. The emergency fund should be a higher-interest account, probably one that can't be accessed with a card, but one that you can easily and quickly move over to your savings account should the need arise. If you are saving for any near-term goal, you might also have a term deposit/CD.

His Way Jose

(ARS = Argentine pesos)

Savings Account:	ARS 170,000
Overseas account 1:	USD 10,000
Overseas account 2:	EUR 10,000

Jose has diversified out of pesos because he is worried about inflation, and the accounts are overseas due to the risk of currency controls that might prevent him from easily accessing or transferring the funds. Note that he has diversified into a couple of foreign currencies to further spread the risk.

Bunker Barry

Savings Account:	$3,000
High Interest Account:	$10,000

Physical Gold	$5,000
Bitcoin	$2,000
Etherium	$2,000

Bunker Barry is paranoid about the future of all currencies so he is diversifying into cryptos and precious metals. Note that even within those volatile cryptos he is further diversifying. If bitcoin collapses, he still has his Etherium. He also, no doubt, has a radiation-proof basement, a decade's supply of Spam, and enough ammunition to take out the most determined zombie horde.

Remember, it is not essential for most people to diversify more than Steady Jeff does, but if you feel the need, that is how you might do it.

Bonds

There's an easy way and hard way to diversify within bonds.

Hard Way

Find a variety of corporate and government bonds, some short term, some long term, some local, some international, and invest in each yourself. Keep track of their maturity dates and any other relevant changes.

Easy Way

Invest in a bond index fund offered by an outfit like Vanguard or BlackRock (there are others). This fund diversifies across many kinds of investment-grade bonds, both government and corporate, in many locations.

If you invest in a bonds index fund, you needn't worry about which bond is maturing when, because there is no maturity date. You don't need to worry about how reliable the corporate or government borrower is because the fund is well diversified across many investment grade bonds, so the risk is limited. Check the details provided for the fund to ensure this is spelled out – look for the words 'investment grade' and avoid 'high-yield', which means risky.

You go to the website, fill in the form, and invest in a bunch of bonds for as long as you like, in the one easy fund. Maximum simplicity plus maximum diversification.

A potential downside of these funds is that, at the time of writing, some of them are investing in insane government bonds that offer negative rates. However, this is a small amount of the overall investment and doesn't seem to affect returns too badly. I just don't like the idea of it. If you don't, figure out how to invest in individual bonds for yourself, or suck it in and accept the unpleasantness.

Shares and Alternatives

Obviously you need to have a *mix* of shares. Only an adrenaline junky would put his life savings into a single company because it might go kaput. *Diversify*. If you invest in 100 companies, the chances that all of them will close down over the next 30 years are tiny. A disaster like that could only be caused by a nuclear war or massive asteroid striking the Earth, in which case you'll have bigger problems to worry about.

There are three main ways of diversifying your shares: (a) do research and pick a variety of shares yourself according to a stock market investing strategy, (b) invest in an actively managed fund where a professional selects the stocks for you, or (c) invest in an index fund, sometimes called a passively managed fund. In this last one a friendly robot blindly invests your money in the whole market. For example, if Vladivostok Fish Concern is 3% of the market, the robot will automatically put 3% of your money into Vladivostok Fish Concern without bothering to consider how good an investment VFC might actually be at the time.

I thought about including a long explanation of why option (c) is best for almost everyone, but then I thought, why bother? This argument is totally settled. Trust me, go with the index fund. End of story.

What, you're still not convinced? You don't trust me? Fine. Read on for the details, but I really think that at this stage in history the evidence is in. If you do believe me, feel free to skip ahead to 'diversifying within alternative growth assets'. And bless you. We'll be right back after this information box about indexes (or indices, if you must), which have already been mentioned several times and might be puzzling you by now:

Stock Market Indexes

We already learned about some of the stock markets around the world. An 'index' is something that measures the change in such a market. An 'index fund' invests broadly in order to match the performance of that index.

Are you with me? No? Okay, here's an example:

One of the most well-known indexes in the world is Standard and Poor's 500 (S&P 500). It follows the 500 largest, publicly-listed companies in the United States, which covers about 75% of the trade there. The S&P 500 rises and falls with the market, showing what is happening overall. Some stocks will rise while others fall, but the index can give us an overview. It does this by assigning the market an arbitrary number, and then records in point form whether it has risen or fallen.

The S&P 500 takes into consideration how large each stock is, or its 'market capitalization'. That means movements in the value of big companies will make more of a difference than the movements of small companies. It is a 'weighted' index.

An index fund uses such an index as a benchmark. That is, it attempts to match the performance of that market overall. More about this soon. First, here are some of the other main indexes:

Dow Jones Industrial Average (DJIA)

This is one of the oldest indexes. It tracks thirty, mostly blue-chip stocks listed on the New York Stock Exchange and the NASDAQ. It is not weighted in the same way as the others and it's very narrow, but it's such a classic that the financial media still follow it, perhaps for old time's sake. The pros tend to pay more attention to the larger and more logically weighted S&P 500.

NASDAQ Composite Index

You might remember that there's a US stock market called the NASDAQ. Well, this is an index that tracks 3,300 equities traded on the market. The companies listed do not have to have their headquarters in the US to be included.

This index is tech-heavy, so the performance of the FAANG stocks (Facebook, Apple, Amazon, Netflix and Google) make a big difference to its overall performance. They constitute around 27% of the total index.[66]

NASDAQ 100

Like the above, but guess how many equities this one tracks? Anyone? Yup, it's a hundred of the largest, most actively traded stocks.

Nikkei 225

Tracks the top 225 blue-chip stocks in Japan. Often just called the Nikkei.

Hang Seng Index (HSI)

An index that tracks the largest companies on the Hong Kong Exchange.

Financial Times Stock Exchange Group (FTSE 100)

This is the weird one you've heard in the financial news when they mention the 'Footsie', and you think it's something about fooling around under the table. It tracks 100 blue-chip companies on the London Stock Exchange.

Other indexes

There are many other indexes, like the ASX 300 which follows the 300 largest companies on the Australian Securities Exchange, the S&P TSX, which tracks the Toronto Stock Exchange, and the S&P NZX, which tracks the 50 largest New Zealand stocks.

Summary

An index is a measure of change in a stock market. It shows whether the market is going up or down, and by how much. It is these indexes that give us the graphs and points we see on TV.

Now when you hear the financial news, it will sound a lot less like gobbledygook and you can impress friends and lovers with your vast knowledge.

Having said that, you don't need to follow such news. If you're investing in shares for the long term, daily movements make no difference. You do need to understand indexes in order to understand how an index fund works, however, and that's coming up next.

Do you know who can pick stocks well enough to beat the average market return, i.e. that which a dartboard, a monkey or an index fund could do? You know who?

Almost nobody, that's who.

Sure, some people can beat it for a year. Some, for several years in a row. But the guy who can beat it over and over again, for decades, is very rare. In fact, he'd be a celebrity. In fact, he is. His name is Warren Buffet, he lives in an old house and he thinks he should pay more tax. And even he has not been doing that well lately. And finally, he himself recommends index funds for the average investor like you.

Of course, I'm being a little facetious. There are other people who are clever and talented enough to beat the market. But they are few. Are you really one of them? Do you have any idea how recent unrest in the Middle East is likely to impact oil prices, and how this might flow on to consumer confidence in the US? Have you factored in how changes in Chinese currency policy might affect the electronics market? And what about how self-driving cars might influence wages in developed countries?

If you really think you know as much about these issues as any professional who calculates the odds full-time for a living, maybe you've got what it takes. Alternatively, you might be an expert in one particular area of the market, say, gaming software, and therefore you might know what's a hot investment in that area. In this case it might be worthwhile, but if you're only investing in gaming software companies then your portfolio will lack diversity. What if the whole gaming market slumps? It could happen.

In general, picking your own stocks takes a lot of time and effort in research and monitoring, and all this hassle only brings you higher risk and not much prospect of a higher return than the market average.[67] Do yourself a favor and use that time to work on a side hustle instead, as discussed in *Step 5: Increase Your Income*.

If you really, really want to get into DIY investing, I recommend you put most of your money into an index fund anyway and use 10% of it to play the market. And if you get really good, and choose to directly invest all your money, and make a fortune, and keep on beating the market over a twenty-year period, good on you. Write me a letter and tell me how stupid I am.

I don't expect to get too many letters.

Now, the discussion thus far assumes you'd be investing in shares for long periods of time. That would be a good idea. There is a whole other field of speculative investing that involves rapidly buying and selling shares for short-term gains. As mentioned earlier, it is called day trading, and almost everybody loses at that game.

If you pick your own stocks for long-term investment and diversify broadly then you'll probably make around the average market return or a bit under, in the long run, despite all that extra effort. On the other hand, if you get into crazy speculation then you might lose the lot.

Why Actively Managed Funds are Bad

Imagine this: your toilet is blocked and you can't fix it yourself so you call a plumber. The plumber has a look and says, "Hmm . . . I'll have a go. I can probably fix it. My fee is $250, or $350 if I succeed." Are you happy with this deal? Most people would expect to pay only once the plumber has fixed the problem, though if it requires more time, personnel or machinery than first thought, then the expense will necessarily be higher. But one would not expect to pay a plumber who messes around with a plunger for a while, sighs, gives up and goes home.

Or how about a taxi driver who expects a $30 bonus if he actually finds your destination? Or a dentist who wants extra if he manages to pull out the right tooth? Or an air traffic controller who reckons he should get an extra fifty bucks for every plane that doesn't crash?

That's how it is with actively managed funds, sometimes just called managed funds or mutual funds. You pool your money with others into a fund run by professionals. They try to pick the best stocks and get you the highest return possible. They collect a fee for their service, and if they actually get a return higher than the market average (i.e. the return a much cheaper robot or monkey-and-dartboard could achieve) then they get a bonus. That is, they get a fee if they don't do their job and they get a bonus on top of it if they *do* do their job, even if it was dumb luck. Or at least that is often how it works.

Okay, it seems a bit unfair, but if you actually end up with a higher return through using a managed fund, who cares?

Ah, but do you actually get a higher return?

Research suggests almost no funds manage to beat the market in the long run, after fees.[68] They might have a good few years but then regress to the mean – or even perform badly in the future.[69] In other words, the fund manager's success was mostly luck.

There are some clever fund managers who can consistently (i.e. most of the time, over a long period of time) beat the market average. I applaud them. The problem is, and this is *very* well established by now, that their fees tend to eat into the returns to the point that they actually offer a lower rate of return in the long run compared to an index fund. The low fees of the index funds give them a big head start against managed funds, which is why they usually win.[70]

For example, the fictional Adamantine Investment Fund hires a bunch of super brainy geniuses who never had a girlfriend in high school and who know how to invest for a higher return. In 2016, the market average was 11.9%. The masterminds at Adamantine Investment Fund, however, manage to score a total return of 13.3%. Awesome news for AIF investors, right?

Wrong.

Those dorks insist on their fees and bonuses, plus there are the account management fees and so on. All in all, the AIF fees cost investors 1.8%. That's a 13.3% return minus 1.8% in fees = an 11.5% net return, or 0.4% less than the market made.

In the meantime, an index fund with a fee of 0.2% that matches the average market result, 11.9%, will return the investor 11.7%, which is 0.2% more than the managed fund. Why bother with a managed fund, unless you're feeling guilty about picking on those geeks when you were a kid and want to make amends?

Some advisors will try to tell you that no, this one fund is really good, they've had excellent returns even taking fees into account for the past *eight years*! Well, that probably means that they're due for a run of bad luck. Or the geniuses will demand a pay rise. Or they'll leave for a better job or to work alone and someone not as good will replace them. Whichever way you cut it, research consistently shows that managed funds are a poor deal compared with indexing.

There are some advantages to managed funds. They are easy to use. They diversify more broadly than you'd be able to do alone. They are mostly safe and reputable. However, index funds offer all these advantages for a lower price. Let's have a look at those, right after this information box about ethical investing.

Ethical investments

There are some managed funds that endeavor to match your values. These are generally known as 'ethical investment funds'. Some avoid investing in things you don't like, such as weapons, tobacco, abortion services, alcohol, carbon-emitting industries, genetically engineering crops, or whatever. This is called 'negative screening'. Others actively seek out companies doing things you approve of, like developing clean energy or being socially responsible. This is called 'positive screening.'[71] There are some funds that do both.

Read carefully about how exactly the fund chooses to invest, and also check out its main investments. The funds vary greatly. Some Islamic funds avoid compound interest, while some Christian funds avoid pornography. Environmentally-conscious funds might seek out public transport infrastructure companies. Some funds avoid Israeli business due to the controversy over the Occupied Territories. And then there are funds that like to add the term 'ethical' or 'sustainable' to their names but a glance at their main investments shows little difference to a conventional fund. Just because a fund is labelled 'ethical' does not mean that it will necessarily match your specific values.

The returns tend to be comparable to other actively managed funds, but as with those, fees tend to eat into profits. From a purely financial point of view, index funds are better.

I first started my investing journey as a long-haired idealist by investing in a tree-hugging, socially conscious fund. Upon closer inspection, I was surprised to find that a large proportion of the fund was invested in a highly government-subsidized, supposedly educational childcare provider. That provider later went belly-up after its creative bookkeeping was exposed.[72] It was not only that, but also the realization that I was paying enormous fees for this 'management', which prompted me to move to index funds, where I have been ever since.

In the end, you choose where to put your money and what limits you will set. I suggest being realistic: will withholding your paltry amount of money from Lockheed Martin really prevent wars in the Middle East? Will investing in a solar panel company that only survives through government subsidies really save the Earth? And how much are you prepared to spend on high management fees for this conviction?

Why Index Funds are Good

An index fund, sometimes called a 'passively managed fund', is another type of mutual fund like an actively managed fund except that instead of a hopefully clever human, an algorithm does the investing for you. It blindly invests in the whole market, attempting to track a stock market index. Remember those indexes from the box a while ago?

Let's say a hypothetical index fund is designed to track the S&P 500. Many do. If Apple Inc. is 2% of that market, the index fund robot will invest 2% in that company. If Apple's share of the market rises to 3%, the algorithm will raise its investment to 3%. And so on. Or at least, it approximately does this, and it repeats the process for enough other stocks so that the performance of the index fund will end up being almost exactly the same as that of the index it is tracking. Different index funds track different stock market indexes, or combinations of indexes.

This is important to note: an index fund attempts to *match*, rather than beat, the market. If the average return of the market one year is 11.9%, a good index fund ought to make 11.9%, too. If the market falls 3.8% over the year, your index fund should also fall by 3.8%. The idea is that the average return, over the long run, is pretty good (maybe 8% or so), and that achieving more than that is impossible for most of us anyway.

Check the fine print to see exactly which index, or group of indexes, a fund is tracking. There ought to be some data provided so that you can confirm how closely it is matching for yourself. If the actual performance is too far off the 'benchmark' (the index that it is supposed to be tracking), there must be something wrong.

The one big, big advantage of index funds is that they offer low fees. Seriously low. They vary, but some offer rates of 0.35% for amounts over $100,000. In the US, Vanguard's fees can be far less than even that. Index funds are by far the cheapest and easiest way to invest in shares.

There are various index funds around, and there are more options in some countries than in others. Personally, I like the flexibility_of Vanguard's selection, and the prices are very competitive. Go to www.vanguard.com and you'll be redirected to their main page. If you are American, this is your website. If you are not, scroll down to the bottom and click on the 'Non-US Investors' option to find the Vanguard site for your country. Hopefully there is one. If not, you might need an advisor to help you find something suitable (see *Step 9*).

Check what products they have available in your country and compare with other index funds. You might find another that suits you better or offers lower fees. However, Vanguard was the best I could find in Australia. I get no kickback from those guys. If anyone from Vanguard is reading, please contact me if you'd like to give me one.

Does something ring a bell? It ought to. Back when we were talking about diversifying bonds, I showed you that the easiest way to do this was to buy an index fund of many bonds from a provider like Vanguard or BlackRock. And now, to diversify your shareholdings, you can basically do the same thing: pick out a suitable index fund of shares from the same provider.

Recap of Stock Diversification

Picking your own stocks is time consuming and very few do well out of it. Actively managed funds have high fees. Index funds, also called passively managed funds, are cheap and easy to use. They are by far the best option for most investors. ETFs are the same thing but can be easily traded online.

After that lengthy discussion about diversification, it turns out that all you need to do is go to a website, pick out suitable share and bond index funds, and put your money into them according to the risk profile that you figured out earlier. There's a little more to know, but you've already got the basics at this point.

I told you it would be easy.

Vanguard Index Funds Available (Retail)

Australia: A cash fund, a bond fund, a property fund (REIT), two Australian stock funds, two international stock funds, and four diversified funds.[73]

Canada: Thirty domestic and international stock funds, five diversified funds, plus some actively managed funds.[74]

New Zealand: NA. Follow the link at the endnote for alternative ways to invest in Vanguard.[75]

United Kingdom: Six UK bond funds, four European bond funds, seven international bond funds, five UK stock funds, six European stock funds, 23 international stock funds, and sixteen diversified funds (including 'targeted retirement'). There are also some active funds.[76]

United States: Eight money-market funds, 36 US bond funds, four international bond funds, 35 US stock funds, 20 international stock funds, 24 balanced (diversified) funds and eighteen alternative/specialty funds.[77] Some of these may be actively managed; I did not have time to investigate them all.

Vanguard funds are also available in various other places.[78]

International Diversification

As you saw in the box, there are a vast array of funds offered by Vanguard in some places. However, you'll only need one or two of these funds to achieve all the share market diversification you need, plus perhaps a bond index fund as discussed earlier. Ignore all the weird and wonderful specialty funds.

Should you diversify your shares by investing in overseas stock markets, or stick with those in your own country? For example, take Steve, an Australian investor. Should he invest entirely in the Australian Shares Fund (which tracks the ASX 300), or should he also have some exposure to the International Shares Fund (which tracks several major indexes for overseas stock markets)?

On the pro side, diversifying internationally would help to hedge your bets in case your home country suffered a downturn. Further, if you plan to retire abroad, global shares will help with currency hedging – if your home country's currency falls, your foreign shares will rise in value against that currency, because they are denominated in different currencies and then converted when you withdraw.

On the cons side, overseas funds might further complicate your investments. If you know that you will retire in your home country, foreign shares can become a currency risk: if your own currency rises, those shares will fall in value for you. Some might also worry about investing in poorly regulated environments. Another consideration is that the more index funds you own, the higher fees you will pay.

Americans should note that foreign stocks tend to be more volatile than their own.

If you are an American, you can possibly get away with holding all-US funds because companies listed on the S&P 500 do a lot of their business abroad, anyway.[80] If you live in a smaller country with a less diverse economy, you would benefit by putting a quarter to a third of your shareholdings into overseas markets. The classic case would be Australia, where the economy is enormously dependent on only two sectors – resources and finance. In addition, the only foreign market exposure you're really getting is China because of the huge proportion of trade with that country.

Some diversified funds already include a mix of local and international shares. If so, you're all set. If not, you might need to purchase two funds, one for local shares and one for international shares. More on these diversified funds later.

Sometimes funds offer 'hedged' or 'unhedged' versions of the international shares product. Wot dat?

The 'hedged' one basically buys something like insurance against changes in currency, so that if your currency rises in value, you do not suffer a loss, or the loss may be softened. The downside is that the fund must pay a fee for this, which cuts into your returns. 'Unhedged' means the fund does not pay for protection against currency fluctuations.

If you are investing for the long run as you should be, you might decide you don't need to hedge as you have time to wait out short-term currency fluctuations. If you are risk-averse and such fluctuations make you panic, consider hedging for the sake of your heart health. If you are torn, it may also be possible to take a bet each way and hedge 50% of your international holdings.

As for the safety of foreign stock markets, don't worry too much about your money disappearing into the lawless badlands of Venezuela or Eritrea. No offense to my Venezuelan and Eritrean readers, but you know what I mean. Most foreign investment, including from index funds, is directed towards developed countries with strong rule of law, and the single biggest destination for foreign investment in the world is the United States. So much for foreign capital taking advantage of Third World countries – their bigger problem is they don't get enough of it.

Some index fund providers diversify a little into 'emerging markets', which means those less developed countries. If this is a small percentage of a diversified fund, that's okay. They'll only put the money into the safer options out of those countries. In fact, some funds have only recently expanded into China, and even there they cautiously keep the amount invested lower than that country's gigantic economy might warrant.

Make sure your fund is set to 'reinvest returns'. That means all the returns you make from dividends and so forth go back into the fund, generating even larger returns in the future through compounding. Having the returns regularly paid out to your bank is most often a strategy for retirees living off their investments, not for someone trying to build their wealth. And as always, make sure you read *Step 9* and get individual advice before making any firm decisions.

ETFs

There's another type of index fund called an Exchange-traded fund, or ETF. Basically it's the same thing except it is easier to buy and sell rapidly online, like an individual share. The fees may differ.

For most people the normal index fund is fine as you shouldn't need to be buying and selling quickly anyway. Remember, growth assets are supposed to be for the long term, hopefully >10 years. In some countries an ETF might be the only kind of index fund available, so you might choose it in that situation. In some cases the fees for an ETF might be lower, which may make it attractive to you.

Curiously, some actively managed funds have started offering their own, cheap, actively managed ETFs in order to compete with index funds on fees. They had to do this because so much money was moving into the latter. I still doubt that these will outcompete index funds net of fees, but I guess you can have a look if it interests you.

Shares Diversification Summary

I hope I've proven to you that index funds are the best way to diversify across different shares. They are superior to both stock picking and actively managed funds because of their reasonable returns and low fees. If you still want to go with one of the other options despite all I've said, fine. If you DIY, make sure you diversify broadly and you'll probably do alright. If you really can't resist testing your financial brilliance against the market, I repeat: put 90% of your growth asset money into an index fund and use the 10% to show off what you can do on your own. It is likely to turn out to be an expensive hobby but at only 10% I guess it won't break the bank.

If you must choose an actively managed fund, look for one with the lowest fees. An extra one percent might not sound like much, but in an extreme case, across 40 years of investing, it could end up costing you $590,000![81] I strongly suggest seeking out low fees before strong past performance as that likely won't be repeated anyway.

Diversifying Across Alternative Growth Assets

This is a simple principle that only requires a paragraph: whatever alternatives you decided to get into, also diversify within that option. For example, if you invest in property, choose a property index fund (REIT) that invests in many properties. These are available from those same outfits like Vanguard and Blackrock. There are also actively managed REITs but, as for shares, these tend to have higher fees. If you invest directly in property, it would be great (though expensive) to have more than one. If laundromats are your thing, it would be best to have more than one, and to expand into automated carwashes or carparks, too. If you're buying the rights to songs, don't put all your money into just one song. Whatever your strategy, diversify across different types of growth assets and also diversify within each category. Don't put all your eggs in one basket.

Reversal

There is such a thing as too much diversification due to the law of diminishing returns. If you are picking shares, two stocks are immensely better than one. Three is better yet, but not by as much, and this pattern continues for the fourth, fifth, sixth and so on. Once you've got twenty stocks, you've reduced your risk by about 70%, and any more stocks over and above that do little more than take up your time and effort to keep track of. Also, with over twenty stocks your return is so diversified that it will likely mirror the index funds – so why bother? Buy the index fund and be done with it. Which is what I recommended anyway.

So long as you're using index funds for shares, bonds and perhaps property, you're well diversified. There's no point in buying, say, a Vanguard index fund and Blackrock index fund that invest in the same thing. It is just extra fees and extra paperwork.

In addition, note that while index funds are the cheapest way to invest, the fees are often structured so that the more of them you have, the more expensive it gets. You can sometimes get a better deal if you invest higher amounts, which means that putting all your money into one fund might be more efficient than spreading it over different funds. Check out the products available and see what makes sense. Most people will only need from one to three funds. Watch out for doubling up, i.e. investing in a REIT fund that is investing in publicly-listed companies you already invested in through your shares fund.

Across all asset classes, unless you're a sophisticated investor with huge funds to manage, there's not much point putting only 1% or 2% into anything. If you might need to use bitcoin for online transactions, fine, have a tiny sliver of bitcoin. If there's no such specific purpose, any investment of under 4% of your wealth might be an annoying complication, not a useful diversification.

As for alternative investments, the sweet spot is where you have a nice mix of assets but are not starting to feel overwhelmed. How many vending machines can you keep track of and pick up cash from? How many carparks can you manage? Once you own a huge number of anything it's going to be an active rather than passive income, i.e. a business, because you'll be spending all your time managing it or managing employees to help you. This is fine if you *want* to run your own business. If not, keep your affairs simple enough to avoid it taking over your life.

A further reversal: if you're running your own business, you may find that it takes up not only all your time, but also all your capital. Sometimes you have to put everything into it to have any chance of success, rather than worrying about diversifying into other investments.

If that is what you choose to do, so be it. Be aware that this is a very risky, but potentially highly profitable, enterprise. You might instead look at diversifying within your own business by, say, expanding your menu or operating over a wider area. Try to put some savings into a pension fund separate from your business. Seek advice. The best of luck to you.

Invest in What You Know?

There is an old piece of advice that says, 'invest in what you know'. For example, if you happen to be a mad keen aviation enthusiast who goes to the airport to take photos of your favorite airplanes taking off, maybe you would be better placed than the average person to know which major aviation companies to invest in.

This is reasonable advice, so far as it goes. However, it would appear to push us in the direction of stock picking, which I spent many paragraphs trying to talk you out of. How can I round the square?

It is not a great idea to only invest in areas of your own expertise because very few people have a broad enough range of expertise to sufficiently diversify their holdings. For example, you can't put all your money in aviation stocks – what happens if the price of fuel rises due to a change in OPEC policy and all aviation stocks plummet at the same time?

This advice would be better put as, 'Don't invest in anything you don't understand'. You will not know much about all the individual stocks in your portfolio if you have an index fund, but it is enough to understand how an index fund works. On the other hand, if anyone ever tries to bamboozle you with a whole lot of impressive words you simply don't grasp – futures, options, puts, derivatives, that sort of thing – then it is best to avoid it.

For that matter, don't even invest in any mainstream products described so far in this book, if, having taken individualized advice, you still don't really understand it. If the description and glossary are still making no sense, look it up online to get more information. Never invest in anything until you've completely got your head around it, otherwise it might not be suitable for you at all.

Some people think it might be a good idea to invest in their own employer, which they know very well, and some companies even expect this. It is not a good idea. Spare a thought for the Enron employees who put all their retirement savings into Enron – then lost both their jobs and their savings once the company went belly-up.[82] This is a classic case of putting all your eggs in the same basket and should be avoided.

More on Diversified Funds

Remember a little while back, we were discussing how you may need a mix of bonds and shares? Well, some of those index funds can help you to do it. Rather than, say, putting 30% of your money into a bonds index fund and 70% into a share market index fund, you might find that there is a 'balanced' or 'diversified' fund available that already diversifies in this way for you. Such diversified funds might also include some cash or equivalents, real estate, or other investments.

An advantage of these products is that you can diversify all you want with one, easy to look after fund. A further advantage is that the larger your investment, the lower the fees tend to be, so by having all your money in one fund rather than spread over two or three, your overall costs would be lowered.

If using Vanguard US, they consistently call these Balanced Funds and there are many options available. Vanguard Australia currently offers four and calls them Conservative, Balanced, Growth and High Growth funds respectively, depending on their mix of shares vs bonds. At Vanguard Canada they come under the 'asset allocation' heading. In the UK you can look at the LifeStrategy or Target Retirement funds. Other countries and companies might have other names, and sadly in some places you'll be hard pressed to find anything like this available at all.

There are a couple of potential downsides to these balanced funds. The first is, you have to choose from their options. In the US you really can't complain because they have so many options you'll be baffled, like when you go to the supermarket and are confronted with seventeen different types of spinach fettuccine. You're going to have to read through the details for yourself, then get independent advice once you've made a tentative choice. In countries where there are fewer options, you might find that you have to choose between 70% and 90% shares when you'd prefer 80%, or accept that they have some exposure to emerging markets when you'd rather not have such exposure, or something like that.

The other disadvantage is that balanced funds give you less flexibility. For example, if for some reason you suddenly need to withdraw $10,000 from a balanced fund that is 60% invested in shares and 40% invested in bonds, you'll effectively be withdrawing $6,000 from the former and $4,000 from the latter. If the share market has plunged, you will realize that part of the loss. On the other hand, if you had separate bond and share funds, you could withdraw all $10,000 from the bonds and avoid realizing any loss on the shares, instead leaving them intact to eventually recover.

Keep in mind that you shouldn't be investing in shares unless you can stay in for the long haul. You really ought to have had that $10,000 in your emergency fund.

Such a lack of flexibility can be a problem for some people, i.e. retirees who are beginning to draw upon their investments, but not for others. Consider your own circumstances and remember to get advice.

For the record, there are also balanced actively managed funds – but you already know what I think of those.

Diversifying Across Time

There is one more risk to consider and it relates to time. Not just time in the market, which we already discussed, but also the time it takes to get in and out of the market.

Theoretically, you might invest all your money in the stock market or real estate at the top of a bull market, or bubble, and then make a sudden loss all at once when the market crashes. I.e., you might have invested in early 2008, right at the worst possible time, and made a big loss in the Great Recession without even having enjoyed the long period of growth that led up to it.

For most of my readers, this is not an issue. Most will invest their money gradually over time – because they don't have much yet! You have to earn and save it first. Making regular investments is actually a great strategy. Earn your money, budget, save, and invest as you go along, over many years, regardless of what the market is doing – exactly as you were going to do anyway. During crashes, if you stick to the plan, you'll automatically be buying more stocks when they are cheap. During a peak, you'll be buying fewer expensive shares. You can ignore the blaring market news and keep investing, month after month. Until you are nearing retirement, it is white noise.

Reversal: if you're lucky enough to have a large amount of money ready to invest for the long term *right now*, you might as well invest the total amount immediately rather than doing it bit by bit. As we have seen, the more time in the market, the better – if the market crashes just after you invest, you will have many years to make it up. The strategy of investing gradually rather than all at once, when you have the option to do the latter, is called 'dollar cost averaging', and research suggests there's not much benefit to it.[83] Time in the market is more important.

Having said that, there's no problem with investing a large amount in a few installments over a couple of months in order to avoid landing right on a market peak.

If you're moving from growth to defensive investments as you near retirement, or for some other reason, consider making this change gradually over time to lessen the risk that you'll suddenly move all your money out of the stock market just after a crash. Selling shares over time spreads the risk out. Usually, as people near retirement, they spend a decade or two moving towards ever greater proportions of defensive assets. However, for most readers, this will be a long way off.

Timing the Market

As briefly mentioned twice earlier, it is tempting, when looking at the ups and downs of the market, to try to time the business cycle so that you buy stocks after a crash when they are cheap, and then sell them after a long bull run, when they are much more expensive.

It sounds like a great idea, doesn't it? Like surfing: wait for a perfect wave that is about to break, and off you go!

Unfortunately, countless studies show that it doesn't work.[84] Even professionals generally fail to pull it off. Yes, we know the market goes up and down, but we don't know *when*. For example, in 2016 everyone knew that the ten-year bull run was getting long in the tooth, everything looked overpriced, and that a downturn must come soon. It looked a lot like the top of the market. Yet in 2019, the market was even higher. If you thought you'd be clever and sell everything in 2016 to skip the inevitable crash, you would have missed out on all that growth.

Similarly, it is hard to pick the bottom of the market. When the stock market crashed in 2008, smart people knew that it would be a good buying opportunity and a terrible time to sell. However, (a) had they saved up a pile of cash specifically for that moment over the last five years, they would have missed out on that five years of growth that had just passed, and (b) they would not know exactly when the market had reached the bottom anyway. They might invest greedily once the market is down 20%, only to see their painstakingly saved wealth suddenly plummet another 30%. In the industry, this is called "trying to catch the falling knife."

If you happen to have some spare cash for long term investments burning a hole in your pocket and suddenly the stock market crashes, fine, go ahead and pour it into your shares index fund if you want to. If stocks are high and you need to move out of the market anyway, feel free. But don't make this your strategy. Only do it if it would make sense anyway, given your broader financial goals. For the most part, ignore what the market is doing and stick to your own plan. And if that plan is the one suggested – making regular investments of your savings over a long period of time – you'll do fine in the long run. Much better than you would by trying to be sneaky and time the market.

I know, it's like finding out there's no Santa Claus. Sorry I was the one who had to tell you.

Investing Conclusion

First we looked at the main types of investments. There are defensive investments like cash, cash equivalents (gold, cryptos etc.) and bonds. These help to protect your wealth and reduce volatility. There are also growth assets like shares, real estate, and the various alternatives listed. These carry higher risk but are essential to building your wealth in the long run.

It is important to diversify your investments. You may choose to diversify between defensive and growth assets if you are nearing retirement or can't handle the stress of stock market volatility. If you are young and don't mind riding the roller coaster of 100% shares, you might not need any cash or bonds at all, aside from your emergency fund and general expenses account.

You also need to diversify within investment categories, especially growth investments. An easy and low-fee way to do this is with index funds.

Many readers will find that they already have some sort of employer retirement plan like a 401(k) or superannuation, and that the advice in this chapter is most useful for choosing between the options within the plan. Others may find that it offers guidance for making their own investments outside of such vehicles. And perhaps the largest group will find that it helps with both.

If you are making your own investments, see how easy it is? You go to a website for Vanguard, BlackRock or whatever is available in your country, and choose the best stock, bond or diversified funds for your own situation. Having read this chapter, you now know what those funds are about and which might be best for you. In fact, if you've made it this far, you already know vastly more about personal finance than the average man in the street.

If you are investing through a retirement program, you are now far better able to differentiate between the options available and pick the one that best suits your own risk profile and investing goals. You'll also spot high-fee managed fund options to avoid.

Before you make any investment decisions, (a) read through all the accompanying documents until you thoroughly understand them, and (b) get advice as per the following chapter. There are a lot of pitfalls when it comes to financial advisors, and I'm going to make sure you know how to get around them.

Retirement Schemes

Developed countries generally have a retirement scheme, or multiple schemes, in order to provide incentives for individual retirement saving and to reduce the burden upon the state pension system.

These vary widely by country, and include the 401(k) and IRA, both Roth and traditional versions (in the US),[85] personal pensions (the UK),[86] the RRSP (Canada),[87] or superannuation (Australia[88] and New Zealand[89]).

Normally, the big carrot dangled in front of your nose is that putting money away for retirement via these schemes can save you a lot on tax. Sometimes the income going into these schemes is not counted as part of your income, and therefore goes untaxed. In some situations the withdrawals are also untaxed, or attract low taxes. Some schemes offer a government or employer co-contribution, which means they may match your payments into the system, in whole or part. And finally, Australia had the brilliant idea of making these payments compulsory, which I guess is even more effective than a tax incentive.

We shall not describe in detail all the retirement programs for each Anglophone country as that would be a book in itself – indeed, it would be a very large book. In fact, you could write a whole book about each nation's retirement system. I encourage you to research your own scheme thoroughly online, then get advice.

In general, there are pros and cons to each of these programs. The pros having already been stated, let us look at some of the cons:

- You cannot access your money until you reach a certain age, or at least not without suffering a financial penalty. This is not the vehicle for money that you may need before retirement.

- The government sometimes moves the goalposts by changing the rules on you, perhaps by altering tax laws or the age at which you can begin to withdraw funds. I am not aware of any egregious changes to personal pensions. In fact, some reforms have improved the situation for retirees. Nevertheless, be aware that the situation may change.

- Generally, pensions are kept separate from the company's other finances. In addition, employees are among the first in line to receive what is owed to them if a company goes bankrupt.[90] Some pensions are also insured. However, check that these safeguards are present in your own jurisdiction, and keep all paperwork related to your pension scheme.

- One of the biggest and most irritating disadvantages these retirement plans can suffer is that they limit your ability to determine where your money goes. You previously would not have worried much about it, but now that you know why low-fee index funds are so much better than high-fee managed funds, you'll be pretty annoyed if you find out that your scheme is primarily invested in the latter. Look around and see what your options are. Most readers will have at least some choice if they are proactive.

A huge problem with all these schemes is that most investors, having been plonked in them automatically, are far too passive. They pay no attention to their pension fund until they are a few years away from retirement, and so are put in the 'default' option which might be unsuitable. In other cases they take no notice of their fund until they hear there's a stock market crash in the news, and then panic-sell everything, thereby realizing a significant loss.

Don't be passive. Be active! Research your current pension fund online, if you have one. See how your money is invested and how high the fees are. Investigate your current investment settings and whether you can change them. And as always, get advice before making any decisions.

I would also suggest keeping at least some of your long-term investments outside of these programs, for the extra flexibility and diversity, even if you have to cop a higher tax rate to do so.

Step 9: Get Advice

No man is so wise that he can afford to wholly ignore the advice of others.

James Lendall Basford

By now you should have approximately worked out where you'd like to invest your money for the long term, based on your individual preferences and risk profile. You'll need to consult a financial advisor to ensure that the plan best suits your individual circumstances. Advisors sometimes have access to financial products that you can't access as an individual, and they can guide you on tax and other issues. Most importantly, a good advisor will be much more expert than I am. They have actual qualifications, you see. So get advice.

You might be wondering, why write a whole book about finance if you're just going to tell me to see a financial advisor at the end anyway? Couldn't I have skipped the book and let the professional tell me what to do?

No.

You see, there are all sorts of problems with this industry. Consider what happened the three times I've received professional financial advice in my life:

On the most recent occasion the advice was good. The advisor explained how my investments would be taxed in my case, being a foreign resident, and this helped to confirm that the path I was pursuing was appropriate for my situation. However, this advisor didn't bother recommending his usual products to me as he realized from our conversation that I was canny enough to know that my existing investments were of better quality. He wasn't indexing, you see.

On the previous occasion, the advice I received was middling. I got some good tips about how to manage currency risk through holding international shares but also was encouraged to consider, yup, another one of those danged blessed high-fee managed funds.

The very first time I received advice it was poor indeed. The advisor recommended against paying off my student loans early, even though I was being offered a 10% discount for doing so. That is called 'free money' and you should seize any such opportunities – there are no other investments that offer a *guaranteed* 10% return! He also discouraged me from putting extra funds into superannuation, even though at that lower income level I would have been getting a matching government co-contribution for doing so. Again, never leave free money on the table.

Instead, the advisor recommended margin loans (remember, that means geared investments, or borrowing to buy shares) that would have caused me to lose everything had the stock market crashed. And this was in . . . 2006, two years before the market did just that.

If I had followed his advice I would have lost everything, and perhaps ended up in debt. My cautious nature saved me. I didn't know much about investing at the time, but I was just clever enough to realize I didn't really understand what he was talking about. I did some independent research and prevaricated long enough to end up taking a different path. He also recommended disability insurance that I realized I already had through a cheaper provider, and he ought to have known that.

Unfortunately, he was probably recommending these inappropriate products to me because they were in his interests, not in mine. I assume he was getting some sort of commission for each one he sold, regardless of whether they suited the customer or not.

> **Here there be tygers!**

Reading this book will empower you to get the best advice, to use that advice properly, and to recognize when someone's taking you for a ride.

Common Problems

These are the common problems you are likely to encounter:

1. Some advisors get a commission (basically a kickback) for referring investors to specific funds. That was probably why the advisor described above was recommending inappropriate margin loans. For example, if your advisor recommends that you put $100,000 into the high-fee, hypothetical Adamantine Investment Fund, he might score a 1% commission if you go ahead with it. That's $1,000. Worse, this might be a trailing commission. That means he gets 1% for *every year* that you're in the fund. Five years later you may have increased your AIF investment to $200,000 and that advisor from ages ago who you've totally forgotten about is still helping himself to $2,000 every year!

That is unfair, it is overly expensive and worst of all, it provides an incentive for your advisor to recommend AIF when another option might be better for your individual circumstances. In other words, he might consciously or unconsciously put his own financial interests ahead of your own. That's what such incentives do. Why else would they exist?

In some cases you can cease the commission after a certain time, but many people are too financially illiterate to even realize that they are still paying.

At the time of writing, such commissions are legal in some countries and illegal in others. Even if they have been prohibited, you might run into the following problem:

2.   Some advisors also get commissions for referring you to specific types of insurance. Perhaps this is why my first advisor was recommending insurance that I already had. The problem is the same as above – a commission provides the advisor with an incentive to recommend insurance that you don't need or which is inferior to what you've already got. Advisors sometimes also get commissions if you change policies, so they encourage you to 'churn' through different policies when you'd be better off sticking with the same one.

3.   Advisors, especially free ones who work for large institutions like banks or mutual funds, are often expected to recommend products offered by their own institution, even if these are not in your best interests.[91] For example, XYZ Bank might expect their advisors to offer customers the most appropriate product offered by . . . XYZ Bank (or its subsidiaries that go by other names). In many cases this advice is okay, but may not be the very best advice you could receive. It is likely to only be the most appropriate out of the institution's own products. Another, outside product might be better for your circumstances, especially if it offers lower fees. Independent advisors (i.e. ones not working for a big bank or other organization) who are free to recommend the services of any institution can often find you a better deal.

4. This industry also contains some downright charlatans. Of these, there are two main categories. The first are unlicensed con artists who are trying to pinch your money. The second are licensed but unscrupulous providers, some of whom work for big institutions. For example, there was a scandal at a major Australian bank some time back with advisors recommending inappropriately high-risk products to customers, and even falsifying documents to make it happen in some cases. This and other rumblings eventually led to a Royal Commission which uncovered all sorts of wrongdoing by the big banks.[92]

How to Proceed

I've hopefully convinced you that it is not a good idea to wander into the office of your nearest financial advisor, turn your brain off and do whatever they say, any more than you would tell a new barber, 'Do whatever you like!' But now you may instead be thinking, financial planners are scary! They'll take all my money! I'd better stay as far away from them as possible!

Relax. Some financial advisors are excellent, most are satisfactory and only a few are downright dodgy. Here is a step-by-step guide for finding a good advisor and for getting the most from their services:

1. Look for proper, licensed providers. Most countries have some kind of register:

In the US, go to https://www.sec.gov/check-your-investment-professional. States are also involved in regulating this sector so check their websites, too.

In the UK, try www.financialplanning.org.uk/wayfinder.

In Canada, fill out the form at https://www.iafp.ca/findaplanner_detailed.php. The main registration page was down at the time of writing.

In Australia, go to www.moneysmart.gov.au/investing/financial-advice/financial-advisers-register.

In New Zealand, go to https://www.fma.govt.nz/investors/getting-financial-advice/finding-an-adviser/.

Just because they're licensed doesn't mean that these advisors are awesome. However, this simple step will at least protect you from some of the unambiguously dishonest con artists who might aim to pinch your money, as many of them will hopefully have been banned from practice for their earlier misdeeds, or were never properly registered to begin with.

2. Look for a purely fee-for-service advisor. That is, seek an advisor who asks for a fee upfront instead of getting a commission. This can be expensive – about 1% of your assets under management (AUM) or a flat fee of $1,000 is not unusual – but it can definitely be worthwhile. First, they ought not to have incentives to push you into commission-paying funds or insurance policies, and so will feel free

to suggest whatever products they really think best suit your needs. Second, if the fee is all upfront, you will know exactly what you are paying, and it will almost always be less in the long run than paying those awful trailing commissions for inferior products.

3. Find an independent advisor. Advisors who work for big institutions are often expected to recommend that institution's own services. I'll give a little reversal to this later on.

4. Be prepared. Don't wander in like a stunned mullet and ask, 'Duh, what do I do about, like, money and that?' Bring along your budget, a list of investments if you already have some, your questions (more on those below), and your goals. Be ready to explain all this clearly and confidently.

5. Interview a few advisors – at least three. The initial meeting is usually free and is a chance to ask some basic questions and get a sense of each other. Choose the advisor who you trust and who seems to be on the same wavelength as you.

6. Be highly cautious of any advisors who (a) push speculative, get-rich-quick schemes, (b) recommend geared investments or any complex financial instruments that you've never heard of or don't understand, or (c) who seem in any way shifty. Go with both your brain and your gut on this. Never invest in something you don't understand, and if you notice these danger signals, run away. As mentioned earlier, some complex and risky products can only be marketed to 'sophisticated' or 'accredited' investors – if you are reading this book, you are not one of those. I suggest avoiding

signing any legal statement saying you are a sophisticated investor, and also avoid the advisor that recommends you do so.

7. Ask questions. During the initial meeting you should ask:

a)   What are your clients like?   Are there others in approximately my situation?

Someone who specializes in high net worth investors might be unsuitable for you if you're not one, as might an advisor who mostly focuses on sorting out debt problems if you don't have any. Some advisors won't even take you on if you don't have enough money, so this might be a good thing to figure out over the phone or via email before you arrive.

b) How do you charge?

Remember, an upfront and one-off fee is good, even if it is high. An ongoing fee to manage your affairs can be acceptable as long as you understand it and agree to it, but make sure they do actually meet with you once a year or so to review your investments – sometimes the cheeky monkeys take the money for this service but then do nothing more for you! This is called 'fee for no service' and was a big problem identified in that Australian banking scandal mentioned. Commissions, especially trailing commissions, are bad. I would almost say, don't even bother getting advice from someone being paid on commission.

(c) Are you free to offer any products? What kind of products do you generally recommend?

If they mention index funds or other sensible products, that is a good sign. Be cautious if they prefer actively managed funds or other high-fee products. Ask them why, then refer back to my rather vitriolic argument on this issue and decide for yourself.

If you find an advisor who seems suitable, explain your financial situation and goals in as much detail as possible. Go through your debts (if any) and where you are with paying them off, your living expenses, your emergency fund, your short and long-term goals, and your ideas for getting there, i.e. how you're thinking of balancing growth and defensive investments. This should be pretty straightforward if you've worked through this book like you were supposed to.

Be sure to discuss your plan's tax-effectiveness. This is one area where jurisdictions and individual circumstances will vary wildly, and where professional advice can be of enormous benefit.

Ask about the relative merits of national or employer retirement savings schemes like the ones mentioned in the box earlier. Ask about the plan's tax effectiveness, how it invests, whether you can change, when you can withdraw, if it would be safe if the employer went bankrupt, and most importantly of all, how high the fees are. Of course, you will have already tried to figure this out for yourself from the website, but now is a chance to check and confer.

Generally, an index fund will charge less than 1% per annum in fees – often way, way less, especially if you invest larger amounts – so if any product is costing you more than that, you need to ask why. I suspect that the answer will be inadequate. Anything that will cost you more than 2% in fees is a joke and your advisor is a clown.

Usually, once you move on to paid advice, your advisor will provide you with a written Statement of Advice which will explain exactly what they recommended for your situation. This is mandated in many jurisdictions. It is a legal document so keep it safe. If you think you've been diddled then this will help back you up. It also protects the advisor because if a client complains, this document ought to show that all advice was demonstrably in the customer's best interests.

8. Cool off. Don't jump straight into the products recommended. Look over the advice again later, research it all online, and consult trusted friends or relatives for an alternative point of view. Only go ahead once you're satisfied that it is the best plan for your circumstances. If, even after reading this book, you still don't understand the advice, don't invest until you do. It is okay to walk away. If you don't understand a product and the advisor says, 'Relax! It's risk free!" you should still say no.

9. If you think you have received poor advice or have been ripped off then you may be able to seek remedy through the relevant body in your jurisdiction. Try those registers of financial advisors for each county listed above or search for the relevant authority online.

10. If you've found a great advisor who's put you on to good, low-fee products that perfectly suit your individual circumstances, be sure to recommend him or her to your friends and relatives. Great advisors swimming in an ocean of mediocre and poor ones ought to be identified and rewarded. But be aware that a good advisor may one day turn into a mediocre one for some reason – I know a case where this happened. Always keep your wits about you.

Reversal

And now for that reversal I mentioned a while back. *If* you are now very confident with your investment skills, you may wish to take a cheaper option – go to one of those big bank/institution advisors and take their free advice . . . with a grain of salt. Consider their suggestions, keep in mind what their incentives and limitations are, compare it with your own research and proceed accordingly.

Financial sections of newspapers, radio shows etc. often provide free, general advice on specific issues for those who write or call in. This may provide additional information if you only need to clarify a particular issue.

Don't hate advisors. They have to make a living, and commissions are often how they do it. The problem is, clients often underestimate the value of good advice and are therefore reluctant to pay what it's worth up front, not realizing that the commissions will cost them more in the long run. Either pay properly upfront or DIY it with some lower quality, free advice to double-check you're heading in the right direction.

Too good to be true?

"If something seems too good to be true, it probably is."

The easiest way to spot a scam is to understand what returns are reasonable, and what returns are not. Here is a quick recap:

Cash: A term deposit or high interest account might provide a safe return of about 2-3% return in normal times, or 6% in special cases such as shortly after the Great Recession began.

Bonds: Investment-grade bonds might return around 4% on average over the long run. Returns are variable, and negative returns are possible, though these are usually limited to a drop of a couple of percentage points.

Shares: The stock market is highly volatile, and may offer a return of around 8% over the very long run. Much higher short-term results are possible, but these are *extremely* uncertain as no one knows what will happen day-to-day. The prospect of suffering a loss over periods less than a decade is high.

Real estate: Returns are perhaps comparable to the stock market over the long run, though somewhat less volatile. Here again, returns are highly uncertain, especially in the short term. It is possible for prices to fall.

Alternative investments: There is *no* type of safe investment that will reliably outdo any of the conventional asset classes listed. None. Zero. Zilch. 0. Nought. 零. Nuffin'. There might be a *risky* investment that offers more, but a safe one? **NO**.

Someone offering you a 'safe' investment that offers significantly higher returns than these is either (a) misleading you about how risky it is, or (b) taking advantage of your avarice to rip you off. For example, there is no product on this blue Earth that offers a *safe* 15% return. Maybe in some alternate universe, but not in ours.

I urge all readers to listen to the podcast linked at the endnote about a notorious conman who deceived friends, partners and others for many years, in many countries, with outlandish promises like these.[93] I hope that understanding how charming and determined he was might help to inoculate you against others like him. In addition, it is very interesting.

Remember the basics: you can only obtain financial freedom by living within your means, saving, and consistently investing over the long run. Trying to increase your income to generate some extra capital to invest is far more sensible that trying to achieve unrealistic returns on your investments.

Don't be greedy. Don't be foolish.

Robo-Advisors

While it's cute to imagine a robo-advisor as an actual, 1970s sci-fi style robot sitting in an office, wearing an adorable tie around its thick, metallic neck, and giving you financial advice in a camp C-3PO voice, disappointingly it is just a glorified financial calculator. You plug in your data through a survey and an algorithm spits out suggestions based on your circumstances. These are sometimes called 'automated investment advisors' or 'digital advice platforms', but 'robo-advisor' sounds much cooler, so let's stick with that.

Robo-advisors are generally very cheap, can offer advice even when you have very little money to get advice on, and are offering increasingly complex advice as the technology develops. Unlike a human, they are available 24 hours a day so long as you have an internet connection. They give you less flexibility than one of those old-fashioned humans because you usually can't get advice on picking individual stocks and bonds, but I tried to talk you out of doing that anyway back in the last chapter.

Three of the biggest robo-advisors are Betterment, Wealthfront and Personal Capital. There are many others. Some of those online calculators I linked to earlier are kind of like mini-robo-advisors, in that they only complete a single function. A proper robo-advisor will bring many such algorithmic processes together that will provide the investor with a more complete service.

Robo-advisors are unable to cope with unusual situations that are not written into their algorithms, nor are they yet able to cope with very complex arrangements that high net worth individuals might have such as tax or estate management. Obviously they will not understand emotional issues that most human advisors will grasp more easily.

The robo-advisor is limited in how well it can survey customers. For example, it will ask about your risk profile: low, medium or high? First, that's rather blunt to start with, and second, some investors will not understand what it means. You'll get it, because you've read *Step 8*, but others will not.

The verdict: robo-advisors may suit beginning investors who have fairly simple financial affairs but who nevertheless already understand the basics of investing. In other words, precisely the target audience for this book, but only once you've finished reading it and have completed the initial steps.

If you really want to save money and won't miss the human touch, consider using a robo-advisor to get you started in your investment journey. Once you've built up some wealth and things are beginning to get complicated, you might want to upgrade to a meat-based application – unless by that time the technology has advanced so rapidly that the robo-advisor will still be good enough. Who knows.

How Good (or Bad) Are Financial Advisors?

An article in *Forbes* magazine suggests that good advice might be worth an extra 3% return per annum or by more than 20% increased retirement savings, including improved tax efficiency.[94] It seems very hard to put a definite figure on it because it would depend on many variables, not least how well the client might have done without that advice in the first place. If he had read this book and made educated decisions, perhaps not such a huge amount. If he hadn't read this book, was not already aggressively paying off debts, had no budget or emergency savings, and was about to put 100% of his cash into junk bonds some guy was selling him over the phone, then the benefits of getting good advice would be spectacular.

Another piece of research suggests that financial advisors, through their own misguided beliefs, often fall into five errors:

1. Chasing past performance. Remember the box about that a little while ago? Past performance is not necessarily an indicator of future performance, and whatever has shone like a thousand suns over the previous five years might stink like a gasoline stand toilet over the next five.

2. Focusing on actively managed funds. Remember how I got stuck into them at some length? The fees are too high; index funds are better.

3. Chopping and changing investments too frequently. Remember how I said to stick with volatile growth assets for the long term? The next chapter explains when you should and should not change investments.

4. Not diversifying enough into international shares. I told most of you to do that, too.

5. Related to 2. above, choosing products with high fees.

After all fees and charges were accounted for, those who had an advisor were doing *about as well* as those who didn't.[95]

But don't despair. A lot of those let-down clients probably lacked financial literacy because they did not read this book, or one like it. When *you* go in for your preliminary meeting with a potential advisor, you'll see for yourself if he is falling into these traps. If he is, find yourself someone else or go robo.

Just because your advisor is wearing an Armani suit and has a compelling, Morgan Freeman voice and authoritatively graying hair, that does NOT mean that he must be right and you must be wrong. You know all about paying off debt, diversification, index funds, and identifying good advice. Don't be afraid to *use* your knowledge. You should be pretty confident by now, because you know nine tenths of everything you need to know for reaching financial freedom.

Let's conclude by working through that final tenth of money wisdom.

Step 10: Record and Reevaluate

The Stock Market is designed to transfer money from the Active to the Patient.

\- Warren Buffet

Recap

You've now done all the basics like budgeting, paying off debts, and setting up an emergency fund. You've moved through setting financial goals, figuring out how to invest, and getting good advice.

What's next?

Before we introduce the final step on this journey, a word of advice: all those earlier steps must be *permanent* if you are to reach financial freedom. You always need a budget, until the day you die. You always need to keep your emergency fund topped up. You always need to avoid bad debt. You always need to get advice before making any major changes to your investments.

It is by maintaining these strategies, and *not* by earning a high income, that you can achieve financial freedom. If you one day earn a much higher income than you do today, it will all be for nothing if you cannot keep up those techniques you've battled through over the last nine chapters. Mess them up, no matter how much you earn, and you'll end up right back in debt.

Keep in mind those wealthy celebrities who went broke that we discussed right back in the introduction. Don't be the next Mark Twain – in your financial affairs, that is. Don't be like 50 Cent, who filed for bankruptcy in 2015 despite massive earnings throughout his career. Even if your income is modest, you can be financially free by diligently following all the steps in this book.

With that said, it's time for *Step 10: Record and Reevaluate*. This will probably be the easiest step of all, if you've worked through the other nine steps properly. You need to know where all your money is, and you need to review your financial affairs on a regular basis. Let's deal with each of these in turn.

Record

You need to keep track of where your money is, because if you've diversified your investments like you were supposed to, things will get slightly complicated.

The simplest possible way would be to write it down and keep the document somewhere safe. This will work fine, and has been done for millennia to great effect. Don't lose it, and keep a copy in a different place. Obviously you can keep a copy saved on Word, too.

Such a document might look like this:

My Investments

Scase Bank at-call savings account:	$3,245
Scase Bank high interest account:	$15,000
Bitcoin:	$5,000
Acme Index Funds: Diversified Bonds	$20,000
Acme Index Funds: Local Shares	$60,000

Acme Index Funds: International Shares	$20,000
Total	**$123,245**

The second way you could do it is by building a spreadsheet on Excel or similar software. If you are familiar with such programs then you will already know that this allows you to set up all kinds of calculations such as totals and subtotals, automatic percentages, and you can color-code it however you like. I do it this way.

I set three cells to tell me what percentage of my money is in cash, bonds and growth assets, respectively. I mark a cell red if I need to top it up (i.e. if my emergency fund gets too low), green if it is good, or orange if I'm planning on moving money out of it. I also have a cell that tells how much I could potentially live on per month at 4% of the total. A spreadsheet also enables you to easily generate charts that help you to visualize what's going on with your money. For example, you can create a pie chart showing how much of your money is in each asset.

If you haven't used spreadsheets much before, there's no need to go out and do a whole course on it, though I guess you could if you wanted to. You can play around with it on your own, use the built-in tutorial and help menu, and see if you can figure it out for yourself. If even I can use spreadsheets, how hard could they be?

The third way to keep track of your investments is to use an app specifically designed for this purpose. Do you remember how we talked about budgeting apps back in *Step 2*? Some of those, like Mint, can also be used to manage your investments. There are plenty of others available. Have a look around and see which one works for you.

Whether you keep track of your investments on paper, on a spreadsheet, or on a dedicated app, make sure that any major changes are duly recorded so that your data is reasonably up to date.

We'll now look at how to use this recorded data.

Reevaluate

How often should you review your investments and consider whether you need to make alterations?

Once a year, or when your circumstances change, i.e. you have quintuplets or you lose both your legs in a lion-taming accident. Fiddling with it any more frequently than that will probably be a waste of time and effort, and might be counterproductive. A watched pot and all that. Feel free to examine your investments frequently, but if you *change* them more than once or twice a year, you're playing with them. Hands off!

Investments work best if they are long-term and you don't chop and change them too frequently, especially your growth assets. Only modify your plan if you have a really good reason to do so.

Good Reasons to Change Your Investments

1. To rebalance. This is a fancy word but the concept is easy enough to understand. Let's look at an example:

If your asset allocation strategy is to hold 20% in bonds and 80% in shares, you might sometimes find that the stock market has had such a good year that your shares have grown to 90% of your total investments, with your bonds now languishing back at 10%.

Assuming your plan is unchanged, you need to move some money from the share fund over to the bond fund until they're back at your intended 80/20 split. This is called 'rebalancing'.

Here's another example, to make sure you've got it. Let's say you have the same 80/20 split but the opposite happens – there's a stock market crash. When it comes time to review your investments, you find that your shares are now down to 60% of your investments, while your bonds are up to 40%. How do you rebalance? That's right, you move some of your money from bonds into shares until you get back to your original 80/20 split. It is that simple.

If you're with Vanguard, download the 'change of investments form' on their website, fill it out, and send it in via mail or fax. In some countries you may be able to do it all online. It depends on local regulations. In any case, it's a once-a-year, fifteen-minute job.

Please note that diversified funds which hold both shares and bonds, like the Vanguard balanced funds mentioned a while back, will do this for you automatically. For example, if your diversified fund holds 80% shares and 20% bonds, and shares shoot up, the fund will automatically rebalance so that your investment will remain at its planned 80/20 split. If you hold this type of fund, you don't need to rebalance yourself. Continue to review your investments yearly to see how things are going.

It is tempting here to think, hey! Shares are going great! Why on Earth would I want to move money out of there?

This is a classic rookie error. Just because the market did well last year doesn't mean it will necessarily do well this year. Don't try to read the future in a crystal ball because you don't have one. Stick to the plan. Remember, don't chase past performance because it is not necessarily an indicator of future performance.

In fact, if shares have shot up over the last year, that is a good time to sell a few while they're high and pick up some more bonds. If shares have declined, it is a good time to buy more by moving money over from your bonds, because the shares are cheap. No brainpower is required here, no timing, and no grand strategy: rebalance annually (or so) and it will all happen for you, as if by magic.

If you have chosen a 100% shares investment strategy for now, there's no need to rebalance. As you get older and near retirement, you will need to take on some defensive assets and that's when you'll start to rebalance annually.

Before we continue, a reminder: we were listing good reasons to change your investments during your yearly review. Let's look at the next one:

2. Your risk profile has changed. For example, if you've been tossing and turning in your bed worrying about a stock market crash, consider decreasing the percentage of your wealth in shares and increasing the amount in bonds and cash. Or if you're suddenly thinking that you're happy to take on more risk, do the opposite. Don't make such a change on a whim. Think it through carefully. You don't want to be switching back and forth all the time according to your shifting mood – pick a plan and stick with it.

3. You might change your investments if your goals have changed. For example, if you've fallen in love, gotten married and knocked up your wife (hopefully in that order), then you might be looking at saving for a deposit on a home. This will obviously mean reconsidering your investments, i.e. setting up a new CD/term deposit for some of your savings. Life will change, and your investments must change with it.

4. If there's something wrong with an asset that you hold, i.e. you realize the fees are too high, or an index fund is not following the

market as it is supposed to, or if you picked your own stocks like I told you not to and a company you bought has been caught out in a nasty scandal, those are all good reasons for changing your investments.

5.   If the investment itself has changed.   For example, I noticed recently that a diversified fund offered by my superannuation company had changed from a growth to a primarily defensive strategy. If you were aiming for growth, it would be reasonable to switch in that situation.

On another occasion I noticed that a high-interest bank account's interest rate had sunk from around 6% to 3%. In a third case, I saw that property had been dropped from a diversified index fund.

Check up on all your investments yearly and see if they are still doing what you think they are doing. Read over investment strategies and fees. Every now and then you'll find that something is no longer suitable.

6.   Finally, if a good financial advisor gives you sensible advice about changing your investments, you might as well pay attention. Because why else are you paying him?

If you make any major changes (i.e. not just normal rebalancing), get advice and consider shifting your investments gradually rather than all at once.

Bad Reasons for Changing Your Investments

There are two really, really bad reasons for changing your investments. They are: (a) panic, and (b) greed.

The most common is panic.

Investors, even otherwise intelligent ones, are very prone to panic. It happens like this: say you have $300,000 in an index fund. Something like the Great Recession occurs and your fund loses . . . oh, I don't know, let's say a third of its value. Now you're down to $200,000. Things are looking grim. Everyone else is panicking, selling everything they own, running around screaming, waving their arms about and putting their underwear on their heads. What are *you* going to do?

If you answered 'nothing', congratulations. That is the correct answer. Sit on your bottom and enjoy the chaos as you might a fireworks show or the demolition of an old apartment block. Wait long enough (perhaps some years) and the value of your fund will eventually be back where it was, and soon after that it will hopefully start growing again. You would actually lose nothing, like Thad in our earlier example.

If, on the other hand, you panic and sell like everyone else, and put whatever wealth you have left into a good, solid bank account, where does that leave you? Well, that leaves you $100,000 out of pocket.

Don't change your investments because of panic. If you have some spare cash lying around, consider doing the opposite of what everyone else is doing: stay deathly calm and actually *buy* shares. Don't try to time the market by saving up for a crash, but if shares are cheap and you happen to have the money at hand, why not?

Reversal: if your investment has suddenly fallen in value even though you thought that it was a safe, defensive investment, that might be a good reason for getting out. If shares fall, you ought to expect that and not worry about it. If your bank is not paying back your term deposit/CD in full, that is a problem. If you feel that you have been misled or mistaken about how risky a product is, it may be worth your while to get out of there quick even though you must realize a loss to do so. It might be a case of cutting your losses. I am reminded here again of those Australian farmers who were tricked into highly volatile investments: they probably should have gotten straight out as soon as they realized how risky it was, instead of believing their advisors that everything was going to be fine and then losing the lot.

The second bad reason for changing your investments is the opposite of panic: greed, and the euphoria that goes with it. If the market is going gangbusters, people are making money hand over fist, and all the financial news people are saying, 'The good times will never end!' you will be tempted to take out that 20% or whatever it was in defensive investments like bonds and put it all into the stock market.

The problem with this is, just because the market has been going well doesn't mean it will continue to do so. Some people actually see this euphoria as a sign of trouble and start to go defensive. I would not recommend this as it is timing the market, which, as we discussed at length, does not work.

Plod along, make your regular investments as usual, rebalance according to your plan yearly, and you'll do better in the long run than you would by trying to chase the rainbow of past performance.

For that matter, don't succumb to peer pressure. If all your buddies are buying bitcoin and making a mint, that does not mean that you should do the same. Reread the section above on crypto, decide what part it should play in your overall strategy, and stick to that plan.

That phrase keeps coming up: *stick to the plan*. This is what should always do when it comes to investments, unless one of those good reasons for changing comes up.

A further note on greed: be very wary of anyone who claims they can get you returns way above what's presently feasible via the assets described in this book. If it's some kind of hedge fund or weird investment with a purported, very high return, it *must* be risky. This is a law of nature. If they claim to have inside information about some asset that's about to go gangbusters, either (a) this is insider trading, which is illegal, or (b) it's a fib.

This book has clearly outlined what kind of returns are feasible in the long run. The main reason that people manage to lose *everything* is that they try for more, fly too close to the sun, and plummet back to Earth.

Don't be greedy.

Summary

You might occasionally change your investments but this should be annual rebalancing or in response to specific, personal circumstances. If you're doing any more than minor adjustments every year then you're fiddling. Stop it, or you will go blind!

Do not change your investments out of panic or greed. Stick to the plan. Patience is the final key to achieving financial freedom.

Conclusion

In the truest sense, freedom cannot be bestowed; it must be achieved.

- Franklin D. Roosevelt

Let's finish by recapping each step and figuring out where you are and what you still need to do.

Review of the Introduction

Many people lack any level of financial freedom, even if they have a relatively high income, because they are unable to manage their money. They live paycheck to paycheck, borrow heavily, and an unforeseen incident can cause disaster. They feel that they are on a treadmill that they can't get off, even for a moment. Many wealthy people have had to file for bankruptcy because they could not get their finances in order.

By following the steps in this book, you can achieve a much greater degree of independence and financial freedom.

There are different levels of financial freedom. Level 1: you are out of debt and don't need to fear a financial emergency or losing your job. Level 2: you could afford to take a year off work if you wanted to. Level 3: you would be able to work part-time or on-and-off. Level 4: you only have to work if you choose to. Level 5: rich.

This book explains how to reach Levels 1-4, but sadly not Level 5. Did you figure out which level you are aiming for, and in what timeframe? If not, think over this some more. Many people merely want to reach Level 4 in their old age so that they can enjoy retirement, and that's fine if that is your goal. Remember, existing government pension and other benefits must have an asterisk after them due to unsustainable public sector debt in many countries.

Step 1: Don't Get Into (More) Debt

You should avoid buying consumer items on credit, and instead save up cash for big purchases. We listed some possible exceptions to this rule.

Are you now living within your means, or are you still living on credit? If you are borrowing for any everyday living expenses, reread this chapter and make the necessary adjustments. You must avoid getting into debt (aside from those exceptions) in order to achieve any level of financial freedom.

Step 2: Make a Frugal Budget

We looked at how to manage your weekly or monthly expenses, and I recommended some apps that make this easy to do.

Have you got a budget figured out? Have you adjusted so that you're now able to put more into savings, or into debt repayments if applicable? If not, you must go back and figure out how to put together a budget. This is the step too many people neglect, and it is probably the primary cause of people's lack of financial freedom.

Step 3: Save an Emergency Fund

This chapter explains why you need an emergency fund, how much it should be, and where you should save it.

Do you have readily available cash to live on for three months if you are still in debt, or six to twelve months if you have no consumer debt, in case you lose your job or face some other catastrophe? If not, you cannot reach Level 1 of financial freedom, and any unforeseen problem could knock you back into debt.

You cannot skip this step, nor can you put it off. If you have already started putting your money into long term investments but do not have an emergency fund, pause your investing immediately and complete this step first.

Step 4: Get Out of Debt

We looked at how to list all your debts in order and pay them off systematically, starting from the one with the highest rate of interest. For those struggling, there are debt counselling services available in various countries that can help you to get your situation under control.

Have you paid off your debts, or sorted out a good plan for doing so? If not, you need to go back and complete this step, otherwise you will not get any closer to financial freedom.

Remember that a mortgage can be an exceptional case depending on your circumstances.

Step 5: Increase Your Income

We went over ways you might be able to increase your income. Some suggestions were conventional while others may have been surprising. Did you succeed in making an extra buck?

While this step is not essential, increasing your income is the most powerful way of reaching financial freedom faster, so long as you're using it to increase savings or debt repayments, not to increase spending. Reread the chapter if you'd like to see those ideas again and reassess whether you might be able to try some yourself.

Step 6: Protect What You've Got

Most people will need some forms of insurance to protect themselves in the case of problems that your emergency fund will not cover. Remember to get professional advice, as covered in *Step 9*, before you take out any policies.

Step 7: Plan Your Life

This is where you figure out what your financial goals really are, aside from just to avoid getting evicted from your home or getting roughed up by Tony the Bulgarian.

Do you have short or medium-term expenses you need to save for, like a car for work or deposit on a home? Have you figured out your long-term goals, especially for retirement? If not, go back to this chapter and think about it again. Use the calculators listed there to help.

If you don't know where you're going, you may be going in the wrong direction. Make sure you are clear about your goals, while accepting that they will probably change over time.

Step 8: Invest Wisely

This gargantuan chapter covered a lot of ground. We considered your 'risk profile' – how comfortable you are with volatile assets. We described the main forms of investment and their various alternatives. To review, these were:

Defensive assets

- Cash and equivalents: cash, precious metals, and cryptocurrencies. These are generally safe but offer lower returns, with the exception of cryptocurrencies which are still jumping around all over the place.

- Bonds. These offer higher but still moderate returns.

Growth assets

- Shares and real estate. Alternatives include peer-to-peer lending, royalties, laundromats and various other things. These investments can offer higher levels of return but at a higher risk, and should be held for the long term (many years) so that you have time to ride out any loss in value. Such growth investing over a long period of time is essential for reaching higher levels of financial freedom.

Diversification

You need to diversify across these asset classes, and also within them. Don't put all your eggs in one basket. Younger people or those more comfortable with risk should lean more towards growth assets. The risk-averse or those nearing retirement should lean more towards defensive assets. Most people will find that index funds will suit them best.

This is the chapter most people will need to reread in order to get their heads around it. Remember to seek individual advice before making any investment decisions.

Step 9: Get Advice

We looked at the potential benefits and pitfalls of getting professional financial advice. Advisors who work on a fee-for-service basis are far better than those working on commission. Advisors working for big institutions may have conflicts of interest. Robo-advisors are also available, cheap, and may be suitable for beginning investors.

If seeing a human, find an advisor that suits you and watch out for the warning signs described. Reread this chapter before going for a meeting with an advisor and write some notes about what you need to discuss.

Step 10: Record and Reevaluate

Keep a record of your investments, either on paper, in a spreadsheet, or using an app like Mint. Review your investments about once a year. Make changes if you need to rebalance or if your situation has changed. Do not make changes out of panic or greed.

Final Words

How did you go? Are you lying on a beach yet, or have you calculated that you should be within a reasonable period of time? Or if you had other financial goals, are you well on your way? Wonderful! Have an extra pina colada for me.

There is always more to learn about personal finance. I thought I knew everything because I'd reached Level 3 of financial freedom already, but my knowledge improved by conducting research for this book. This is good news for you: if I reached Level 3 in about a decade by grasping the basics, then imagine how well you'll do with even more information at your fingertips! The learning journey never ends, for any topic. Check out the links below as a jumping-off point for your own further reading.

Having read this book, you are better educated about personal finance than 95% of the general public. Maybe 98%. By putting these steps into action, you *will* move towards higher levels of financial freedom. It takes time and discipline, but now you are moving in the right direction instead of running on the spot with debt, overspending, a lack of emergency funds, and high-fee investments.

I wish you all the best in your financial future and I hope you achieve everything you dreamed of. If it takes a while to get there . . . well, you'll appreciate it all the more once you arrive.

If you found this book useful, please recommend it to someone else who needs to get his head around money. Also, I would greatly appreciate it if you could leave an honest review on Amazon or wherever you bought this book.

To celebrate your journey towards reaching financial freedom, let us conclude with one more quote:

Freeeeeeeeeeeeeeeeedom!

- William Wallace, *Braveheart*

Links and Further Reading

Links provided in the book

Debt related

Calculate the real cost of your debt:

www.bankrate.com/calculators/managing-debt/annual-percentage-rate-calculator.aspx

How long to pay off debt calculator:

www.calcxml.com/calculators/pay-off-loan?skn

Debt counseling:

US: www.usa.gov/debt

Canada: creditcanada.com/

UK: www.moneyadviceservice.org.uk/en/tools/debt-advice-locator

Australia: www.moneysmart.gov.au/managing-your-money/managing-debts/financial-counselling

New Zealand: https://www.fincap.org.nz/

Budget related

Budgeting apps:

www.mint.com

www.youneedatbudget.com

Budgeting/minimalist websites:

mrmoneymustache.com

www.theminimalists.com

Find lost/unclaimed money

US: www.usa.gov/unclaimed-money

UK: https://pocketsense.com/unclaimed-money-uk-5264182.html

Canada: www.canadianpersonalfinance.com/finding-unclaimed-money-canada.html

Australia: www.moneysmart.gov.au/tools-and-resources/find-unclaimed-money

New Zealand: https://treasury.govt.nz/information-and-services/other-services/unclaimed-money

Other calculators

Savings calculator for future expenses:

www.msn.com/en-us/money/tools/savingscalculator

Retirement calculators:

www.msn.com/en-us/money/tools/retirementplanner

www.calculator.net/retirement-calculator.html

Interest rate calculator:

www.vertex42.com/Calculators/inflation-calculator.html

Return on investment calculator:

www.investor.gov/additional-resources/free-financial-planning-tools/compound-interest-calculator

Index funds

www.vanguard.com (there's a longer URL but you'll be redirected automatically)

www.blackrock.com (as above)

Registers of financial advisors by country

US: https://www.sec.gov/check-your-investment-professional.
States are also involved in regulating this sector so check their
websites, too.

UK: www.financialplanning.org.uk/wayfinder.

Canada: fill   out   the   form   at
https://www.iafp.ca/findaplanner_detailed.php. The main register page
was down at the time of writing.

Australia: www.moneysmart.gov.au/investing/financial-
advice/financial-advisers-register.

New Zealand: https://www.fma.govt.nz/investors/getting-financial-
advice/finding-an-adviser/.

Further Reading
I do not necessarily endorse the content of these websites and
books. It's good to get another point of view.

Websites
Introductory and general information
www.fool.com (take their stock picks with a grain of salt –
remember, I told you not to do that sort of thing anyway)

www.practicalmoneyskills.ca (this one's very introductory if that's where you're at)

www.investor.gov (introductory site for Americans, includes useful calculators and scam alerts)

www.moneyadviceservice.org.uk/en (something very similar offered in the UK)

https://investingintroduction.ca/en/ (mostly for Canadians)

moneysmart.gov.au (mostly for Australians, but with good, basic, and straightforward information for anyone new to managing money)

www.investopedia.com (perfect for definitions of terms that you're struggling to get your head around. I go back to this one all the time.)

Financial independence, retire early (FIRE)

www.apurplelife.com

www.thesimpledollar.com

www.thebalance.com

https://www.getrichslowly.org/

www.madfientist.com (free but requires registration)

Books

A Random Walk Down Wallstreet: The Time-Tested Strategy for Successful Investing, by Burton G. Malkiel. This one is often recommended by finance professionals for beginners, and it explains why indexing is best.

The Total Money Makeover: A Proven Plan for Financial Fitness, by Dave Ramsey. This is largely about getting out of debt, and advocates a somewhat different strategy to the one suggested in *Poor Man's Guide to Financial Freedom.*

The Little Book of Common Sense Investing: The Only Way to Guarantee Your Fair Share of Stock Market Returns, by John C. Bogle. This book advocates and explains the use of indexing in more detail.

The Millionaire Next Door: The Surprising Secrets of America's Wealthy, by Thomas J. Stanley. This book reinforces what I've been trying to tell you: truly rich people don't live in giant mansions and drive flash cars. They live within their means and wisely manage their money, which is how they got rich in the first place.

There are many other titles that I do not recommend. Be wary of any finance book that advocates the very things I warned you about: day trading, currency speculation, flipping houses, borrowing to invest, picking stocks, timing the market, and all the rest of that nonsense. Avoid anything that looks like a 'get rich quick' book. In the real world, slow and steady wins the race.

Glossary

401(k)

An employer-sponsored retirement plan available in the United States. Investment gains are not taxed, and you can also subtract contributions from your income, which may lower your income tax bill. Options vary wildly between plans, some good and some not so good. You can access the funds once you're 59.5 years old unless you're still working for that employer. Americans see also: **Roth IRA**. Australians and New Zealanders see also: **Superannuation**.

Accredited investor – see **Sophisticated investor**.

Actively managed fund

A type of mutual fund where you pool your money with other investors and finance professionals invest it for you. Sometimes they are just called 'managed funds', but this is confusing because passively managed funds, or index funds, are also sometimes called managed funds. The fees tend to negate any advantage you may receive in higher returns.

Bank statement

The letter or email you get from the bank, usually monthly, telling you how much money you have in your account(s) and all transactions in and out of the account. These days you can generally check your account online at any time so you don't have to wait for an official statement, but banks still tend to send them out for regulatory reasons. Check your statements to make sure every transaction is legitimate and that you're not accidentally paying for a service that you forgot to cancel.

Bankruptcy

When you officially declare that you're broke and can't repay your creditors. In civilized countries this usually means that someone will go over everything you have, make you pay back whatever is reasonable by selling off some assets, and then let you go with a black mark against your name for any future borrowing. Get advice before declaring bankruptcy.

Bear market

When the stock market declines in value by around 20%. In a bear market, the prices of all shares tend to fall, even those that might have good potential for future earnings. It is a time of pessimism among investors. Never panic during a bear market. Stick to your plan. Compare: **Bull market**. See also: **Recession**.

Blue chip stocks

Shares in big, stable companies that have been around for a long time. They often pay out reliable **Dividends**. Blue chip stocks tend to be more expensive than shares in newer, smaller companies. If you have an index fund this will give you exposure to all types of shares, including some blue chip ones.

Bonds

Bonds, also called fixed income, are loans made to companies or governments for a fixed annual amount of interest (called the 'coupon rate') and for a fixed period of time, after which the bond will 'mature' and the debt will be repaid, hopefully.

A bond has a 'face value', or what it will be worth once its fixed period is finished. However, the bond can be sold on to a third party, and the price in such a case can vary from the face value according to interest rates, market sentiment about the ability of the borrower to pay up, and other factors. The borrower might also repurchase the debt, say, if they think they can now reissue bonds at a better rate.

If the official interest rate rises, the price of bonds falls. If the interest rate falls, the price of bonds rises. The price of a bond is inverse to its 'yield', which means the amount of interest it pays relative to its real, rather than face, value.

For example, say there is a bond with a face value of $100 with a 2% coupon rate (that's interest, remember). If the price of the bond falls to $90 due to rising interest rates, it still pays out $2 per annum. Two dollars from $90 is a yield of 2.22%, instead of 2%.[96]

All this is of mostly academic interest for the average investor. The main thing to know is that bonds generally have a return and level of risk somewhere between that of cash and shares, so long as they are 'investment grade' bonds. Debts issued by less reliable borrowers are called 'high yield' or 'junk bonds', and should be avoided by non-sophisticated investors.

Budget

A detailed plan of how you will spend each dollar, broken down into categories such as rent, groceries and fuel. The idea is that you can identify ways to spend less and thereby increase your savings or debt repayments.

Bull market

A time when the prices of all shares tend to rise. Even poor companies with underlying problems can enjoy a boom during a bull run. It is a time of optimism among investors. Compare: **Bear market**.

Capital gain

When you make money because something you own increases in value. If the price of your house or shares go up, those are capital gains. In most countries you will need to pay tax on capital gains once you realize them, i.e. sell the asset.

Cash

This is plain old money that is not invested in shares, bonds, real estate etc. It might be physical banknotes in your wallet or it might be in a bank account. Cash is low risk and often easy to use at short notice but it has a lower return on investment (sometimes none at all) compared to other forms of investment.

CD – see **Time deposit**

Collateral

An asset that a borrower puts up as security for a loan, and which can be seized by the lender to recover some or all of the amount owed if the borrower does not come up with the cash. For example, you might pawn an old ring. If you can't repay the loan, the pawnshop sells the ring. Another example is a mortgage – if you can't meet your obligations, the bank can seize the house.

Commission/trailing commission

A kickback to an advisor or other person who refers you to a particular financial product like a managed fund or insurance. A trailing commission is when this payment continues for as long as you hold the product. Most financial dictionaries would not use a term so negatively loaded as 'kickback', but I like it for that reason – commissions give advisors incentives other than your best interests.

Compounding

Interest on interest, or returns on top of returns. Say you invest $100 in a term deposit and get 2% interest per year. The second year you actually get 2% interest on $102, not $100, because of the interest you made in the first year. Nice, hey? But unfortunately the same thing happens when you borrow money – the amount you have to repay compounds and can increase alarmingly over time.

Consumer item

Something you purchase to use, not as an investment. A jet ski would be an example of a consumer item. A house would not, as it can retain or increase its value over time.

Correction

When the price of a security or market falls by at least 10%. It means that the price was probably too high given realistic forecasts of future earnings, and that it is now closer to its 'correct' level. If the whole market falls more than 20% over two quarters, this is the point where some analysts will start calling it a **Bear market** rather than a correction.

Credit score/rating

A measure of how good you are at paying off debts. If you've paid them back in the past then computers have noticed this, and they tell potential lenders that you're good for the money. If you don't pay back money on time then you'll have a bad credit score and lenders might insist on a higher interest rate or not lend to you at all. Having a good credit rating means you can borrow more easily and cheaply.

You'd think that taking ages to pay back debts and only paying back the minimum each month would give you a bad credit rating, but it doesn't. So long as you're meeting your obligations, this actually makes you a pretty good customer because lenders will get more money out of you in the long run.

Creditor

Someone who lends money. For example, if the bank lends you money for a car, the bank is your creditor.

Crystalized profit/loss – see **Paper profit/loss**

Debit card

Like a credit card, but it uses your own funds directly from your bank account rather than borrowing money. It can generally be used wherever credit cards can be used (online purchases etc.), but you have to actually have the money. Which is good, because that makes it harder to live beyond your means. A debit card does not usually offer the same reward programs as credit cards.

Debt consolidation

A form of debt refinancing that involves taking out a loan to pay off your other debts, effectively rolling all your debts together into one big debt. Seek advice before doing this.

Debtor

Someone who owes money. For example, if you borrow money to buy a car, you are a debtor.

Default

When you do not meet the obligations of your loan. That is, you do not pay back the agreed amount at the agreed time. Even being short on one payment puts you in default, which wreaks havoc on your credit score.

Defensive investment

An investment aimed at protecting your wealth, usually offering a lower return on investment than riskier options. **Cash** and investment-grade **Bonds** are generally considered defensive.

Deflation

When prices in general fall over time. This is rare but not unheard of. Compare: **Inflation**.

Diversification

This means investing in many different assets rather than one asset or a small number of assets.

You can diversify across types of investments, for example, cash, bonds, shares and real estate. You can also diversify within a type of investment, i.e. by choosing a large number of shares rather than a small number.

Diversification helps to manage risk because the chances of all investments failing at once are low.

Dividend

Sometimes a company pays out some of its profits to shareholders. That's called a dividend. You can also make money from shares if they increase in value. If you're investing in shares through an index fund and reinvesting then this isn't something you really need to think about – the bot will take the money and reinvest it in more shares for as long as you hold the fund.

Emerging markets

The economies of developing countries such as China, India and Brazil. Depending on the options available in your country, it may be possible to choose some exposure to emerging markets through an **Index fund**. Emerging markets can offer additional diversification but they tend to be highly volatile. While such markets can grow rapidly, they can also collapse suddenly. Also keep in mind that economic growth in an economy might not be mirrored by growth in the index of the main share market in that country, because a lot of businesses might not yet be listed on the stock exchange.

I suggest that the rookie investor not exceed about 5% exposure to emerging markets. Also consider what your advisor says.

ETF

An exchange traded fund. It's a type of index fund that you can easily trade online. The fees may differ from those of a conventional index fund.

Ethical investing

Investing in such a way as to match your own ethical convictions, be they religious, moral, social or environmental. The term mostly refers to a type of actively managed fund labelled 'ethical' or 'socially responsible'. There are also ethical bank accounts.

False economy

When an effort to save money ends up costing you money instead. For example, if you get the $10 bike lock instead of the $50 one, thinking you'll save $40, and then someone cuts it and steals your $600 bike, that's a false economy.

Fixed income – see **Bonds**

Flipping

When you buy an asset in order to sell it a short time later for a quick profit. The term usually refers to real estate, but people can also attempt to flip individual shares, cryptocurrencies, or anything, really. Scalping tickets is a form of flipping.

Flipping is risky because the price of the asset might not rise within a short time frame as you anticipated. For ordinary investors like us, growth assets ought to be held for the long term.

Foreclosure

If the owner of a house does not meet his obligations to the lender, i.e. he defaults on his mortgage, then the lender can 'foreclose' the property. That means they sell it in order to get their money back, or some of it. Many properties were foreclosed by banks during the **Great Recession** that began in 2008. See also: **Collateral**.

F*** you money - see **Emergency fund**.

Future dollars

The value of money in the future. It will probably be less than the value now. For example, a US stamp used to cost 5 cents, meaning each dollar had a greater value than it has today. Also see **Inflation**.

GDP

Gross Domestic Product. This is the total value of all finished goods and services within a country over one year. It is an approximate measure of the size of an economy and the wealth of a country. You may also see the term Gross National Product, or GNP. Very roughly, it is like GDP but includes overseas earnings.

Geared investments

Also referred to as margin loans or leveraging, it means borrowing money to invest, usually in shares or real estate.

Gearing for shares can increase your profits in a rising market but may increase your losses sickeningly if the market falls. In such a case, the lender will make a 'margin call', which means you have to stump up some quick cash to bring your stake back up to the agreed level. If you don't have the cash, the lender will sell your shares to restore the balance, which is bad for you because they've just lost value and you will realize a loss.

People can lose some serious money with geared share market investments, and you don't need such instruments to reach reasonable financial goals. I recommend that non-sophisticated investors avoid them altogether.

Gearing is probably necessary for an investment property because a house is too expensive for most people to buy outright without a loan. You must keep meeting your mortgage obligations even if you have trouble finding tenants or need to pay for costly maintenance. You'll need a healthy buffer of cash in your emergency fund.

Using your home as collateral for a geared property or shares is very risky because if you can't keep up with the mortgage or receive an unpayable margin call, you may end up losing your own house as well as the investment.

GIC – See **Time deposit**

Global Financial Crisis (GFC) – see **Great Recession**.

Great Recession

Also called the Global Financial Crisis (GFC), it was the economic trouble starting in 2007 when some major banks failed and the stock market fell dramatically. Such events will certainly occur again so take this into account as you determine your level of comfort with risk.

Growth investment

An investment aimed at building wealth, usually entailing a higher level of risk in the short term. Shares and real estate are growth investments. Compare: **Defensive investment**.

Guarantor

A person who promises to pay back a loan if the borrower defaults. Sometimes parents act as guarantors for their children to take out student loans, which they can come to regret. In other cases, a company will act as a guarantor so that you can find accommodation, especially when working overseas in a place where landlords are wary of letting out apartments to dirty, thieving foreigners like us. Cough, Japan, cough.

Be extremely cautious about acting as a guarantor for anyone, as it is a very common way of catching an **STD** (sexually transmitted debt). If someone asks you to sign on as a 'witness' to a loan, read that agreement very carefully before signing, no matter how cute she is. You might be being tricked into acting as a guarantor. If she can't or won't pay, you're on the hook for the whole amount.

Hedge Fund

A managed fund that invests in complex ways in order to hedge against stock market volatility. Such products are only suitable for sophisticated investors.

High interest bank account – see **Money market account.**

Hyperinflation

An extremely high rate of inflation, sometimes defined as more than a 50% increase in the cost of goods and services over a single month. Hyperinflation is rare in developed countries but has frequently occurred throughout history. Cases include Zimbabwe in the 2000s, Russia in the 1990s, and the Weimar Republic (Germany) in the 1920s.

Income

Any money you have coming in. Your salary, rent received from your property, or regular cash gifts from your grandma can all be forms of income.

Index

An index is a measure of changes in a market. For example, the S&P 500 is an index that tracks the five hundred largest companies listed in the United States. The Nikkei 225 is an index that tracks the top 225 companies listed in Japan. Don't confuse the index with the stock market. The latter is where you buy and sell securities, while the former is a tool for tracking changes in the market. See also: **Index fund**, **Stock market**.

Index fund

A type of mutual fund where you pool your money with other investors and an algorithm invests it for you. It blindly invests in the whole market using an index rather than trying to pick winners. For example, if Microsoft is 2% of the market, that percentage of your money will be invested there. Different index funds track different markets. Fees are generally low. Index funds are sometimes called passively managed funds. See also: **ETF**. Compare: **Actively managed fund**.

Inflation

The nasty habit of prices rising over time. You know how your granddad always goes on about how he used to get a McDonalds hamburger for 15 cents? That's inflation for you. You need to hold some growth assets, otherwise your savings will not keep up with inflation and you will gradually lose money over time.

Also see **Future dollars** and **Hyperinflation**. Compare: **Deflation**.

Interest

The cost of a loan. For example, if you borrow $10,000 for a car at 6% interest, you will pay $10,000 plus $600 interest if you pay it back in the first year. If it takes longer to pay back then the borrowing cost will be higher.

Banks may pay you interest to invest your money. The return is usually low but very safe.

Each country has its own, official interest rate, usually determined by a Reserve or Central Bank. This rate will influence all other rates.

Investment

Putting money into an asset in the hope of making more money out of it in the future. Buying a nice car to become an Uber driver is an investment. Buying a nice car to impress the ladies is not.

An investment may require a lot of managing, like a new grill for your chicken shop. A passive investment is one that does not require you to do as much, like shares or a rental property.

Leveraging – see **Geared investments**.

Liquid

Liquid funds means money that's easy to get at if you need it. A savings account is super liquid because you can take it out whenever you want, either for an online purchase or at an ATM. Money tied up in a house is not liquid. You can't use that money to buy something else unless you sell the house, take out a loan against it, or something like that. You need to have adequate liquid funds available in your emergency fund.

Managed fund

'Managed fund' usually refers to an **Actively managed fund**, but can also be used to mean a passively-managed **Index fund**. Whichever fund you're looking at, be sure about which it is and how it invests.

Margin loans – see **Geared investments**.

Money market account (MMA)

No, an MMA has nothing to do with mixed martial arts. It is a bank account that offers a higher interest rate than a normal deposit account, but comes with restrictions such as a required minimum amount and limited monthly transactions. Outside the US, banks might not use the term 'money market account', but if your bank offers a product like this, it's basically the same thing. An MMA is a good place to put your emergency fund. See also: **Money market fund**.

Money market fund

This sounds very much like a **Money market account**, but it's a little different. This is a mutual fund where your money is pooled with others' and used to invest in low-risk investments like **Time deposits** and short-term securities. Money market funds are usually not backed by the government the way money market accounts are, but are nevertheless very safe because they put money into low-volatility investments. This is also a good place to put your emergency fund. Be aware that it may take a few days to get your money out, so keep adequate funds in the bank to cover immediate expenses that may arise.

Mortgage-backed securities (MSBs)

According to Investopedia, "A mortgage-backed security (MBS) is an investment similar to a bond that is made up of a bundle of home loans bought from the banks that issued them. Investors in MBS receive periodic payments similar to bond coupon payments. (. . .) As became glaringly obvious in the subprime mortgage meltdown of 2007-2008, a mortgage-backed security is only as sound as the mortgages that back it up."[97]

Some **REITs** invest in MSBs.

Mutual fund

This means any kind of fund where a group of people put their money together to invest. **Actively managed funds** and **Index funds** are both kinds of mutual funds.

National debt

The total debt owed by a government. Sometimes people use the terms 'government debt' or 'public debt'. These can be used interchangeably or there can be subtle differences, depending on the situation.

In addition, we can refer to 'total' or 'net' debt. Total national debt means what it says. Net national debt is the total debt minus the debts that are owed by others to the country. For example, Japan's total debt is 236% of GDP, but its net debt is 153%. This is because others owe Japan money. Much of this comes from Japan buying up US government bonds, so in effect the US owes Japan money and the second figure takes this into account.

Negative equity

When the value of a property falls below the amount still owing on the mortgage. For example, say you buy a $200,000 house with a $20,000 deposit and a $180,000 loan. Four years later, the housing market crashes and your property is only worth $120,000. Unfortunately, you still owe $150,000 on the mortgage. This means you have negative equity in the house. It is also known as being 'under water'.

Negative return

A loss. For example, if you invest in Vladivostok Fish Concern Pty. Ltd. and the company falls in value, that is a negative return. You lose money if you sell your shares at that moment.

Overdraft

When a bank lets you spend more money than you have in your bank account. This is handy if you lose track of how much is there, but sometimes the interest they'll charge you for the loan amounts to an arm and a leg. As with other forms of debt, using an overdraft should generally be avoided.

Paper profit/loss

A paper profit or loss is when you must actually close, or sell, an investment to realize the profit or loss. For example, if the value of your index fund rises and you sell, you realize the profit. If you do not sell at that time, it is still a paper profit. In the case that the value of the fund falls, you will either make a paper or realized loss depending on whether you sell at that time.

The main relevance here is that you should not panic about a paper loss on a long-term investment. If there is volatility in the market, you should usually stick to your plan and see it out, not panic-sell and realize a loss unnecessarily.

Passively-managed fund – see Index fund

Portfolio

Your set of investments, say, cash, bonds and shares. The word 'portfolio' makes it sound as though you have such a broad variety of them that you need a file to keep track of them all, because you used to get actual, paper copies of the shares and bonds. These days a portfolio can be managed electronically.

Principal

The original amount of a loan. For example, if you borrow $10,000 to buy a car at 6% interest, the principal is $10,000 and the interest is $600 in the first year. You have to pay back both the principal and the interest to clear the debt. The principal stays the same but the interest can quickly stack up if left unpaid.

Private equity

A company that is not publicly listed on the stock exchange. It is not open to everyone to buy and trade its shares. There are other ways of investing in private equity but these are probably more suitable for sophisticated investors.

Realized profit/loss – see **Paper profit/loss**

Rebalancing

Say you plan to hold 20% defensive and 80% growth investments. After a year you find that your growth investments have risen to 90% of your total wealth, while defensive assets have fallen to 10%. Putting some of the money from growth back into defensive investments in order to stick with your original plan of an 80/20 split is called rebalancing. If you hold both shares and bonds, you should rebalance about once a year.

Recession

Often defined as two consecutive quarters of economic contraction, i.e. a sustained fall in **GDP**. It is a time when unemployment rates are increasing and businesses are struggling. Recessions tend to be associated with prolonged **Bear markets**.

Refinancing

Replacing a debt obligation with a new, different debt obligation. This can make sense in some situations, i.e. you're able to borrow at a cheaper price, at a more stable, fixed rate, or Tony the Bulgarian is threatening to eat your turtle if you don't repay your debt tomorrow at 10 a.m. in the parking lot behind the 7-11. Get advice before refinancing.

Reinvest

Say you have a shares index fund and you make a profit of 6% in one year through a combination of **Dividends** and increased share prices. If you put that 6% into more units of the same index fund, then you are reinvesting it. In general, this means ticking the 'reinvest' box when you first purchase the product and then the fund does this for you automatically. If you take the 6% out, you are not reinvesting it.

You've got to choose the 'reinvest' option if you want to take advantage of **Compounding** and actually build your wealth. Often retirees do not reinvest the whole amount because they are using it for living expenses, but they are not my intended audience.

REITs

Real Estate Investment Trust. It is a fund that invests in some form of property. This might include **Mortgage-backed securities**, commercial real estate companies, and others.

Retail investor

A normal investor who is not especially expert, and/or has less than around a million dollars of investable assets. Basically, it is you. Retail investors should avoid overly complex or risky products. Compare: **Sophisticated investor**.

Return on investment (ROI)

How much money you get in return for your investment. For example, if you invest $100 in bonds and they return $4, your return on investment is 4%.

Risk profile

The level of risk you are willing to take on. If you don't mind the wild fluctuations of the stock market, your risk profile is high. If you'd prefer to soften those blows with some defensive assets, your risk profile is medium. If you want to minimize volatility as much as possible, your risk profile is low.

Younger people with a long time to invest should generally take on more risk than older people who will need to draw on their investments for income in the near future, or at the present time. However, your own personality also determines your risk profile. If you can't stomach suffering huge paper losses on your shares, perhaps you should lower your risk profile accordingly.

Roth IRA

A type of retirement plan available in the United States. Unlike a 401(k), it is an individual fund that does not involve your employer. There are more options, the fees are higher, and you can only contribute after-tax income. It is possible to withdraw money from a Roth IRA before you turn 59.5, but you'll incur taxes and penalties.

Securities

A financial instrument that can be traded. Basically it means shares and bonds, although there are additional kinds of securities that do not concern us here.

Shares

Shares (also called stocks or equities) are when you buy a part of a company. If the company rises in value or pays out a **Dividend** then you can make a profit. If it loses value then you make a loss if you sell at that time. Shares have a higher level of risk and potential return than cash and bonds. They are most suitable for long-term investments.

Share market – see **Stock market**.

Sophisticated investor

An investor with a high net worth, usually over a million dollars, or with expertise in investing. Some assets are restricted to such investors. Sophisticated investors may choose risky, complex products that lesser mortals like you and I are better off avoiding.

Speculation

The kind of investment that is short-term, risky, and often depends on a bit of luck. An example would be buying a house in the hope of selling it a short time later for a profit because house prices seem to be rising in the area. The risk is that prices might not continue to rise steadily as you expected them to, and you get stuck with a house that is now worth less than you bought it for.

People also speculate on short-term changes in stock prices, currency fluctuations and a myriad of other things. Unless you are an expert it is basically gambling.

STD

Sexually transmitted debt. It is when you catch a debt from a loved one by acting as a guarantor, sharing a credit card, buying a house together, or marrying/cohabitating with someone who had preexisting debts that you perhaps didn't know about. Sometimes these STDs are inadvertent, while in other cases a mendacious partner might deliberately try to offload hers onto you. If you are getting serious, be open about finances with each other, proceed with caution, and also ensure you don't pass an STD onto anyone else.

Stocks – see **Shares**.

Stock market

The place where **Shares** in companies are bought and sold. There are multiple stock markets. For example, the world's two largest stock markets are the New York Stock Exchange and the

NASDAQ, both in the United States. The third largest is the Tokyo Stock Exchange in Japan. There are many others.

These days stock market trading is pretty much all online. The age of sweaty blokes in garish vests screaming and hyperventilating disappeared along with mullets and roller-skating rinks.

Sometimes the average value of the stock market rises, which means that most investors make a profit. Sometimes it falls, meaning investors suffer a loss. The stock market usually rises over the long term but big falls regularly occur. See also: **Index**.

Stockbroker

Someone who helps to buy and sell shares for you. Some also give advice on what shares you should buy or sell. You don't need one of these to invest in shares through an index fund.

Superannuation

A retirement program in Australia, New Zealand, and some other places. In Australia, contributions are compulsory. A certain percentage of wages is subtracted and invested in a retirement account. Workers can elect to make additional payments. Superannuation reduces taxation but the funds cannot be withdrawn until you are old. Americans see also: **401(k)** and **Roth IRA**.

Term deposit – see **Time deposit**

Time deposit

When you lend money to the bank for a fixed period of time. It is a very safe investment as the return is fixed, but the interest rate tends to be low. Withdrawing the money early incurs costs, so this investment is only suitable for money you definitely will not need until it reaches maturity. Time deposits are a good place to put money you're saving for a goal <5 years away such as a car or a deposit on a house.

Time horizon

How long you intend to invest for. If you are saving for a silver Phantom ring next year then you have a short time horizon and need to put the money somewhere stable like a term deposit or high interest account. If you are saving to retire in thirty years or so then you have a long time horizon and you can afford to invest in more volatile assets like shares.

Unrealized profit/loss – see **Paper profit/loss**

Volatility

How much the value of an investment is likely to jump around. A term deposit in the bank isn't supposed to jump around at all. It's meant to increase by the agreed amount of interest, which will not be much. Short of some highly unlikely disaster, that's exactly what will happen. Shares, on the other hand, are highly volatile. Their value can jump up or down by crazy amounts within a single day, or even within minutes.

Volatile assets ought to be held for the long term – at least ten years, probably longer. This gives you time to recover from sharp downturns.

Wholesale investor

This usually means an institutional investor who is investing huge amounts of money at a time. Some assets are restricted to wholesale investors, and the minimum investor amount tends to be around half a million dollars. See also: **Sophisticated investor.**

Z Tranche

According to Investopedia, "A Z Tranche is the portion of a structured financial product that only receives payments once all the other tranches have been retired."[98]

I have no idea what that means either, but good on you for reading all the way through the glossary. The best of luck with your journey towards financial freedom.

- Nikolai

Endnotes

1 https://www.youtube.com/watch?v=xdfeXqHFmPI
2 https://www.forbes.com/sites/johnmauldin/2017/10/10/your-pension-is-a-lie-theres-210-trillion-of-liabilities-our-government-cant-fulfill/#738a894b65b1
3 https://en.wikipedia.org/wiki/List_of_countries_by_public_debt
4 https://www.businessinsider.com/rich-famous-celebrities-who-lost-all-their-money-2018-5?op=1#t-pain-said-he-went-from-having-40-million-in-the-bank-to-having-to-borrow-money-to-get-his-kids-burger-king-25
5 https://en.wikipedia.org/wiki/Mark_Twain#Financial_troubles
6 https://www.wsj.com/articles/eyeing-that-sweater-its-yours-in-four-easy-payments-11569672000
7 https://www.cnbc.com/2018/09/11/heres-how-to-protect-yourself-fromsexually-transmitted-debt.html
8 https://www.cnbc.com/2018/09/11/heres-how-to-protect-yourself-fromsexually-transmitted-debt.html
9 https://www.amazon.com/Worthless-Aaron-Clarey-ebook/dp/B006N0THIM
10 https://www.asus.com/us/
11 https://budgeting.thenest.com/percentage-americans-credit-cards-30856.html
12 https://www.debt.com/statistics/
13 www.mint.com
14 www.youneedabudget.com
15 https://dqydj.com/sp-500-periodic-reinvestment-calculator-dividends/
16 https://www.nerdwallet.com/blog/mortgages/invest-or-pay-off-your-mortgage-heres-how-to-decide/
17 https://smartasset.com/investing/should-i-pay-down-mortgage-or-invest
18 https://money.cnn.com/retirement/guide/basics_basics.moneymag/index7.htm
19 https://apurplelife.com/2017/12/28/2017-state-of-the-union/
20 https://www.valuepenguin.com/credit-cards/credit-card-spending-studies
21 https://apurplelife.com/2020/03/17/how-pursuing-fire-has-changed-how-i-act-at-work-part-2/
22 https://www.cnbc.com/2018/01/18/few-americans-have-enough-savings-to-cover-a-1000-emergency.html
23 https://www.independent.co.uk/news/uk/home-news/british-adults-savings-none-quarter-debt-cost-living-emergencies-survey-results-a8265111.html
24 https://www.news.com.au/finance/one-in-five-australians-have-no-cash-savings-to-fall-back-on/news-story/0208d50855ce48b0a5aa19fc266a4f0d
25 https://www.valuepenguin.com/average-credit-card-debt
26 https://www.valuepenguin.com/average-student-loan-debt
27 http://money.com/money/5233033/average-debt-every-age/
28 https://www.cnbc.com/2019/05/23/nearly-25-percent-of-americans-are-going-into-debt-trying-to-pay-for-necessities.html
29 https://data.oecd.org/hha/household-debt.htm
30 https://blogs.wsj.com/wealth/2012/02/29/the-new-poster-child-for-class-warfare/
31 https://gettrouble.com/p/noobnichesite/
32 https://www.simplethriftyliving.com/total-amount-unclaimed-money-every-state/

33 https://www.policygenius.com/life-insurance/learn/whole-life-versus-term-life-insurance/

34   https://www.landers.com.au/insights/publications/family-and-relationship-law/de-facto-relationships-and-asset-protection-whats-mine-is-yours/

35 https://www.debt.com/statistics/

36   https://www.biznews.com/thought-leaders/2013/09/10/retire-at-55-and-live-to-80-work-till-youre-65-and-die-at-67-startling-new-data-shows-how-work-pounds-older-bodies

37 https://www.investopedia.com/terms/f/four-percent-rule.asp

38 https://en.wikipedia.org/wiki/List_of_countries_by_inflation_rate

39   https://www.theguardian.com/world/2013/mar/25/cyprus-bailout-deal-eu-closes-bank

40 https://www.nytimes.com/2001/12/03/world/argentina-limits-withdrawals-as-banks-near-collapse.html

41 https://www.investopedia.com/terms/c/cryptocurrency.asp

42 https://en.wikipedia.org/wiki/Bernie_Madoff

43 https://antion.com/top20seminarscams.htm

44   https://www.marketwatch.com/story/here-is-why-your-savings-rate-is-more-important-than-your-investments-returns-2017-07-20

45   https://www.nytimes.com/2009/04/26/your-money/stocks-and-bonds/26stra.html

46   https://www.investopedia.com/ask/answers/042415/what-average-annual-return-sp-500.asp

47 Ibid.

48 https://www.thebalance.com/why-it-is-so-hard-to-make-consistent-money-day-trading-1031238

49 https://papers.ssrn.com/sol3/papers.cfm?abstract_id=3423101

50

https://money.cnn.com/2008/12/18/news/economy/hedge_fund_liquidations/?postversion=2008121817

51   https://observationsandnotes.blogspot.com/2009/04/best-worst-20-years-in-stock-market.html

52 https://www.handbook.fca.org.uk/handbook/COBS/4/12.html#DES582

53 https://en.wikipedia.org/wiki/Accredited_investor

54

https://www.abc.net.au/radionational/programs/backgroundbriefing/macquarie-bank/9811240

55

https://www.unexplainedpodcast.com/episodes/2019/2/16/lhpe4sk7s6q483xq43ww9ws1qy8xch

56   https://captaincapitalism.blogspot.com/2019/04/the-house-on-lake-minnetonka-that-never.html

57 https://www.nerdwallet.com/blog/mortgages/invest-or-pay-off-your-mortgage-heres-how-to-decide/

58 https://smartasset.com/investing/should-i-pay-down-mortgage-or-invest

59 https://propertyupdate.com.au/9-reasons-why-you-shouldnt-buy-an-investment-property/

60   https://www.localagentfinder.com.au/blog/why-use-a-real-estate-agent-to-manage-your-rental-property/

61   https://www.investopedia.com/articles/investing/090815/buying-your-first-investment-property-top-10-tips.asp

62 https://www.macroaxis.com/invest/market/VNQ--compareProfile--%5EGSPC

63   https://www.dummies.com/education/math/statistics/how-to-interpret-a-correlation-coefficient-r/

64 https://jlcollinsnh.com/2014/05/27/stocks-part-xxii-stepping-away-from-reits/

65 https://www.investopedia.com/articles/06/compoundingdarkside.asp

66   https://www.bloomberg.com/news/articles/2018-05-04/faang-stocks-swallow-up-more-of-the-nasdaq-than-ever-before

67 https://www.whitecoatinvestor.com/picking-individual-stocks-is-a-losers-game/

68   https://www.fool.com/investing/2016/08/27/index-funds-vs-mutual-funds.aspx

69   https://www.marketwatch.com/story/why-way-fewer-actively-managed-funds-beat-the-sp-than-we-thought-2017-04-24

70   https://www.thebalance.com/why-index-funds-beat-actively-managed-funds-2466411

71   https://www.choice.com.au/money/financial-planning-and-investing/stock-market-investing/articles/ethical-investing-guide

72   https://www.abc.net.au/news/2008-08-27/fast-eddy-leaves-abc-learning-investors-reeling/490536

73
https://www.vanguardinvestments.com.au/retail/ret/investments/product.html#/productType=retail

74 https://www.vanguardcanada.ca/individual/home.htm

75   https://www.passiveincomenz.com/how-to-invest-in-vanguards-index-funds-while-living-in-new-zealand/

76 https://www.vanguardinvestor.co.uk/what-we-offer/all-products

77 https://investor.vanguard.com/home/

78 https://global.vanguard.com/portal/site/home

79 https://www.blackrock.com/corporate/global-directory

80 https://apurplelife.com/2019/10/29/why-i-own-100-us-stocks/

81   https://www.nerdwallet.com/blog/investing/millennial-retirement-fees-one-percent-half-million-savings-impact/

82 https://www.nytimes.com/2001/11/22/business/employees-retirement-plan-is-a-victim-as-enron-tumbles.html

83 https://seekingalpha.com/article/4067554-dollar-cost-averaging-work

84   https://www.fool.com/investing/2017/04/02/yet-another-study-shows-that-timing-the-market-doe.aspx

85 https://www.fidelity.com/viewpoints/retirement/spender-or-saver

86 https://www.gov.uk/personal-pensions-your-rights

87   https://www.canada.ca/en/revenue-agency/services/tax/individuals/topics/rrsps-related-plans/registered-retirement-savings-plan-rrsp.html

88 https://www.ato.gov.au/Individuals/Super/

89
https://www.workandincome.govt.nz/eligibility/seniors/superannuation/index.html

90 http://www.401khelpcenter.com/401k_education/bankruptcy_and_401k.html

91   https://www.theguardian.com/australia-news/2018/jan/24/asic-accuses-banks-financial-advisers-of-working-against-customers-interests

[92] https://en.wikipedia.org/wiki/Royal_Commission_into_Misconduct_in_the_Banking_%2C_Superannuation_and_Financial_Services_Industry

[93] https://www.theaustralian.com.au/podcasts/podcast-who-the-hell-is-hamish/news-story/c95b519a9ececa6076df80bd130ba158

[94] https://www.forbes.com/sites/wadepfau/2015/07/21/the-value-of-financial-advice/#4bbca2ad1333

[95] https://alphaarchitect.com/2018/11/29/is-financial-advice-conflicted-or-is-it-simply-misguided/

[96] https://www.investopedia.com/terms/b/bond.asp

[97] https://www.investopedia.com/terms/m/mbs.asp

[98] https://www.investopedia.com/terms/z/ztranche.asp

www.ingramcontent.com/pod-product-compliance
Lightning Source LLC
Chambersburg PA
CBHW021350210526
45463CB00001B/49